A test with books open. (Fairhope, Alabama.) *Frontispiece.*

SCHOOLS OF TO-MORROW

BY
JOHN DEWEY
AND
EVELYN DEWEY

NEW YORK
E. P. DUTTON & COMPANY
681 FIFTH AVENUE

Copyright, 1915
BY
E. P. DUTTON & COMPANY

The Knickerbocker Press, New York

PREFACE

There has been no attempt in this book to develop a complete theory of education nor yet review any "systems" or discuss the views of prominent educators. This is not a text book of education, nor yet an exposition of a new method of school teaching, aimed to show the weary teacher or the discontented parent how education should be carried on. We have tried to show what actually happens when schools start out to put into practice, each in its own way, some of the theories that have been pointed to as the soundest and best ever since Plato, to be then laid politely away as precious portions of our "intellectual heritage." Certain views are well known to every teacher who has studied pedagogy, and portions of them form an accepted part of every theory of education. Yet when they are applied in a classroom the public in general and other teachers in particular cry out against that classroom as a place of fads and caprices; a place lacking in any far reaching aim or guiding principle. We have hoped

PREFACE

to suggest to the reader the practical meaning of some of the more widely recognized and accepted views of educational reformers by showing what happens when a teacher applies these views.

The schools we have used for purposes of illustration are all of them directed by sincere teachers trying earnestly to give their children the best they have by working out concretely what they consider the fundamental principles of education. More and more schools are growing up all over the country that are trying to work out definite educational ideas. It is the function of this book to point out how the applications arise from their theories and the direction that education in this country seems to be taking at the present time. We hope that through the description of classroom work we may help to make some theories living realities to the reader. On the other hand, we have dwelt on theoretical aspects in order to point out some of the needs of modern education and the way in which they are being met.

The schools that are used for illustration were chosen more or less at random; because we already knew of them or because they were conveniently located. They do not begin to represent all that is being done to-day to vitalize

PREFACE

the school life of children. Schools with like traits may be found in every part of the country. Space has forced us to omit a very important movement—the reorganization of the rural school and the utilization of agriculture in education. But this movement shows the tendencies that mark the schools we have described; tendencies towards greater freedom and an identification of the child's school life with his environment and outlook; and, even more important, the recognition of the rôle education must play in a democracy. These tendencies seem truly symptoms of the times, and with a single exception proved to be the most marked characteristics of all the schools visited.

Without the very material help and interest of the teachers and principals of the schools visited this book would not have been possible. We thank them most sincerely for the unfailing courtesy they have shown in placing their time and the material of their classrooms at our disposal. Our thanks are especially due to Mrs. Johnson of Fairhope and to Miss Georgia Alexander of Indianapolis for information and suggestions. The visiting of the schools with one exception was done by Miss Dewey, who is also responsible for the descriptive chapters of the book.

J. D.

CONTENTS

CHAPTER		PAGE
I	EDUCATION AS NATURAL DEVELOPMENT	1
II	AN EXPERIMENT IN EDUCATION AS NATURAL DEVELOPMENT	17
III	FOUR FACTORS IN NATURAL GROWTH	41
IV	THE REORGANIZATION OF THE CURRICULUM	60
V	PLAY	103
VI	FREEDOM AND INDIVIDUALITY	132
VII	THE RELATION OF THE SCHOOL TO THE COMMUNITY	164
VIII	THE SCHOOL AS A SOCIAL SETTLEMENT	205
IX	INDUSTRY AND EDUCATIONAL READJUSTMENT	229
X	EDUCATION THROUGH INDUSTRY	251
XI	DEMOCRACY AND EDUCATION	287

LIST OF ILLUSTRATIONS

                                                            FACING PAGE

A TEST WITH BOOKS OPEN. (FAIRHOPE, ALA.) *Frontispiece*

(1) NATURE WOULD HAVE CHILDREN BE CHILDREN BEFORE THEY ARE MEN.
(2) TEACH THE CHILD WHAT IS OF USE TO HIM AS A CHILD. (TEACHERS' COLLEGE, N. Y. CITY) 8

TO LEARN TO THINK, WE MUST EXERCISE OUR LIMBS. (FRANCIS PARKER SCHOOL, CHICAGO) . . . 15

(1) AN HOUR A DAY SPENT IN THE "GYM."
(2) THE GULLY IS A FAVORITE TEXTBOOK. (FAIRHOPE, ALA.) 30

GAMES OFTEN REQUIRE MUSCULAR SKILL, READING, WRITING, AND ARITHMETIC. (UNIVERSITY SCHOOL, COLUMBIA, MO.) 45

(1) THE BASIS OF THE YEAR'S WORK. (INDIANAPOLIS) .
(2) PRINTING TEACHES ENGLISH. (FRANCIS PARKER SCHOOL, CHICAGO) 58

SONGS AND GAMES HELP ARITHMETIC. (PUBLIC SCHOOL 45, INDIANAPOLIS) 75

THE PUPILS BUILD THE SCHOOL-HOUSES. (INTERLAKEN SCHOOL, IND.) 87

REAL GARDENS FOR CITY NATURE STUDY. (PUBLIC SCHOOL 45, INDIANAPOLIS) 97

(1) MAKING A TOWN, INSTEAD OF DOING GYMNASTIC EXERCISES. (TEACHERS' COLLEGE PLAYGROUND, N. Y. CITY)
(2) GYMNASIUM DANCES IN SEWING-CLASS COSTUMES. (HOWLAND SCHOOL, CHICAGO) 108

LIST OF ILLUSTRATIONS

FACING
PAGE

CONSTRUCTING IN MINIATURE THE THINGS THEY SEE AROUND THEM. (PLAY SCHOOL, NEW YORK CITY) . . . 118

USING THE CHILD'S DRAMATIC INSTINCT TO TEACH HISTORY. (COTTAGE SCHOOL, RIVERSIDE, ILL.) . . . 129

LEARNING TO LIVE THROUGH SITUATIONS THAT ARE TYPICAL OF SOCIAL LIFE. (TEACHERS' COLLEGE, N. Y. CITY) . 140

SOLVING PROBLEMS IN SCHOOL AS THEY WOULD HAVE TO BE MET OUT OF SCHOOL. (FRANCIS PARKER SCHOOL, CHICAGO) 159

THE PUPIL STAYS IN THE SAME BUILDING FROM DAY NURSERY THROUGH HIGH SCHOOL. (GARY, IND.) . . . 177

SPECIAL TEACHERS FOR SPECIAL SUBJECTS FROM THE VERY BEGINNING. (GARY, IND.) 193

(1) THE BOYS LIKE COOKING MORE THAN THE GIRLS DO.
(2) MENDING THEIR OWN SHOES, TO LEARN COBBLING. (PUBLIC SCHOOL 26, INDIANAPOLIS) 218

LEARNING MOULDING, AND MANUFACTURING SCHOOL EQUIPMENT. (GARY, IND.) 255

REAL WORK IN A REAL SHOP BEGINS IN THE FIFTH GRADE. (GARY, IND.) 269

(1) CHILDREN ARE INTERESTED IN THE THINGS THEY NEED TO KNOW ABOUT. (GARY, IND.) 284
(2) MAKING THEIR OWN CLOTHES IN SEWING CLASS. (GARY, IND.)

TRAINING THE HAND, EYE, AND BRAIN BY DOING USEFUL WORK. (GARY, IND.) 297

SCHOOLS OF TO-MORROW

CHAPTER I

EDUCATION AS NATURAL DEVELOPMENT

"We know nothing of childhood, and with our mistaken notions of it the further we go in education the more we go astray. The wisest writers devote themselves to what a man ought to know without asking what a child is capable of learning." These sentences are typical of the "Émile" of Rousseau. He insists that existing education is bad because parents and teachers are always thinking of the accomplishments of adults, and that all reform depends upon centering attention upon the powers and weaknesses of children. Rousseau said, as well as did, many foolish things. But his insistence that education be based upon the native capacities of those to be taught and upon the need of studying children in order to discover what these native powers are, sounded the key-note of all modern efforts for educational progress. It meant that education is not something to be forced upon children and youth from without, but is the growth of capacities with which human beings are endowed at birth. From this conception flow the various considerations which educational reformers since his day have most emphasized.

It calls attention, in the first place, to a fact which professional educators are always forgetting: What is learned in school is at the best only a small part of education, a relatively superficial part; and yet what is learned in school makes artificial distinctions in society and marks persons off from one another. Consequently we exaggerate school learning compared with what is gained in the ordinary course of living. We are, however, to correct this exaggeration, not by despising school learning, but by looking into that extensive and more efficient training given by the ordinary course of events for light upon the best ways of teaching within school walls. The first years of learning proceed rapidly and securely before children go to school, because that learning is so closely related with the motives that are furnished by their own powers and the needs that are dictated by their own conditions. Rousseau was almost the first to see that learning is a matter of necessity; it is a part of the process of self-preservation and of growth. If we want, then, to find out how education takes place most successfully, let us go to the experiences of children where learning is a necessity, and not to the practices of the schools where it is largely an adornment, a superfluity and even an unwelcome imposition.

But schools are always proceeding in a direction opposed to this principle. They take the accumulated learning of adults, material that is quite unrelated to the exigencies of growth, and try to force it upon children, instead of finding out what these children need as they go along. "A man must indeed know many things which seem useless to a child. Must the child learn, can he learn, all that the man must know? Try to teach a child what is of use to him as a child, and you will find that it takes all his time. Why urge him to the studies of an age he may never reach, to the neglect of those studies which meet his present needs? But, you ask, will it not be too late to learn what he ought to know when the time comes to use it? I cannot tell. But this I know; it is impossible to teach it sooner, for our real teachers are experience and emotion, and adult man will never learn what befits *him* except under his own conditions. A child knows he must become a man; all the ideas he may have as to man's estate are so many opportunities for his instruction, but he should remain in complete ignorance of those ideas that are beyond his grasp. My whole book is one continued argument in support of this fundamental principle of education.''

Probably the greatest and commonest mistake that we all make is to forget that learning is a necessary incident of dealing with real situations. We even go so far as to assume that the mind is naturally averse to learning—which is like assuming that the digestive organs are averse to food and have either to be coaxed or bullied into having anything to do with it. Existing methods of instruction give plenty of evidence in support of a belief that minds are opposed to learning—to their own exercise. We fail to see that such aversion is in reality a condemnation of our methods; a sign that we are presenting material for which the mind in its existing state of growth has no need, or else presenting it in such ways as to cover up the real need. Let us go further. We say only an adult can really learn the things needed by the adult. Surely the adult is much more likely to learn the things befitting him when his hunger for learning has been kept alive continuously than after a premature diet of adult nutriment has deadened desire to know. We are of little faith and slow to believe. We are continually uneasy about the things we adults know, and are afraid the child will never learn them unless they are drilled into him by instruction before he has any intellectual or practical use for them. If we could really believe that attending to the needs of present growth would keep the child and teacher alike busy, and would also provide the best possible guarantee of the learning needed in the future, transformation of educational ideals might soon be accomplished, and other desirable changes would largely take care of themselves.

It is no wonder, then, that Rousseau preaches the necessity of being willing to lose time. "The greatest, the most important, the most useful rule of education is: Do not save time, but lose it. If the infant sprang at one bound from its mother's breast to the age of reason, the present education would be quite suitable; but its natural growth calls for quite a different training." And he says, again, "The whole of our present method is cruel, for it consists in sacrificing the present to the remote and uncertain future. I hear from afar the shouts of the false wisdom that is ever dragging us on, counting the present as nothing, and breathlessly pursuing a future that flies as we pursue; a false wisdom that takes us away from the only place we ever have and never takes us anywhere else."

In short, if education is the proper growth of tendencies and powers, attention to the process of growing *in the particular form in which it goes on from day to day* is the only way of making secure the accomplishments of adult life. Maturity is the result of the slow growth of powers. Ripening takes time; it cannot be hurried without harm. The very meaning of childhood is that it is the time of growth, of developing. To despise the powers and needs of childhood, in behalf of the attainments of adult life, is therefore suicidal. Hence "Hold childhood in reverence, and do not be in any hurry to judge it for good or ill. Give nature time to work before you take upon yourself her business, lest you interfere with her dealings. You assert that you know the value of time and are afraid to waste it. You fail to perceive that it is a greater waste of time to use it ill than to do nothing, and that a child ill taught is further from excellence than a child who has learned nothing at all. You are afraid to see him spending his early years doing nothing. What! Is it nothing to be happy, nothing to jump and run all day? He will never be so busy again all his life long. . . . What would you think of a man who refused to sleep lest he should waste part of his life?" Reverence for childhood is identical with reverence for the needs and opportunities of growth. Our tragic error is that we are so anxious for the results of growth that we neglect the process of growing. "Nature would have children be children before they are men. If we try to invert this order we shall produce a forced fruit, immature and flavorless, fruit that rots before it can ripen. . . . Childhood has its own ways of thinking, seeing, and feeling."

Physical growth is not identical with mental growth but the two coincide in time, and normally the latter is impossible without the former. If we have reverence for childhood, our first specific rule is to make sure of a healthy bodily development. Even apart from its intrinsic value as a source of efficient action and of happiness, the proper development of the mind directly depends upon the proper use of the muscles and the senses. The organs of action and of reception are indispensable for getting into relation with the materials of knowledge. The child's first business is self-preservation. This does not mean barely keeping himself alive, but preservation of himself as a growing, developing being. Consequently, the activities of a child are not so aimless as they seem to adults, but are the means by which he becomes acquainted with his world and by which he also learns the use and limits of his own powers. The constant restless activities of children seem senseless to grown-up people, simply because grown-up people have got used to the world around them and hence do not feel the need of continual experimentation. But when they are irritated by the ceaseless movements of a child and try to reduce him to a state of quiescence, they both interfere with the child's happiness and health, and cut him off from his chief means of real knowledge. Many investigators have seen how a sound bodily state is a *negative* condition of normal mental development; but Rousseau anticipated our present psychology as to the extent in which the action of the organs of sense and movement is a positive cause of the unfolding of intelligence. "If you follow rules that are the opposite of the established practice and instead of taking your pupil far afield, wandering to distant places, far-off lands, remote centuries, the ends of the

(1) Nature would have children be children before they are men.
(2) Teach the child what is of use to him as a child.
(Teachers College, N. Y. City.)

world and to heavens themselves, you keep him to himself, to his own concerns, he will be able to perceive, to remember, and to reason in nature's order of development. As the sentient infant grows into an active being, his discernment keeps pace with his increase in strength. Not till strength is developed beyond the needs of self-preservation is the faculty of speculation manifested, for this is the faculty of employing superfluous strength for other than necessary purposes. Hence, if you would cultivate your pupil's intelligence, *cultivate the strength it is meant to control.* Give his body constant exercise, make it strong and healthy in order to make him good and wise; let him work, let him do things; let him run and shout; let him be on the go. . . . It is a lamentable mistake to imagine that bodily activity hinders the working of the mind, as if the two kinds of activity ought not to advance hand in hand, and as if the one were not *intended to act as guide to the other.*"

In the following passage Rousseau is more specific as to the way in which the physical activities which conduce to health and the growth of mind reënforce each other. "Physical exercise teaches us to use our strength, to perceive the relation between our own and neighboring bodies, to use natural tools which are within our reach and adapted to our senses. ... At eighteen we are taught in our schools the use of the lever; every village boy of twelve knows how to use a lever better than the cleverest mechanician in the academy. <u>The lessons the scholars give one another on the playground are worth a hundredfold more than what they learn in the classroom.</u> Watch a cat when she first comes into a room. She goes from place to place; she sniffs about and examines everything. She is not still for a moment. It is the same with a child when he begins to walk and enters, as it were, the room of the world about him. Both use sight, and the child uses his hands as the cat her nose.''

"As man's first natural impulse is to measure himself upon his environment, to find in every object he sees the qualities that may concern himself, so his first study is a kind of experimental physics for his own preservation. He is turned away from this, and sent to speculative studies before he has found his own place in the world. While his delicate and flexible limbs and keen senses can adjust themselves to the bodies upon which they intended to act is the time to exercise senses and limbs in their proper business—the time to learn the relation between themselves and things. Our first teachers in natural philosophy are our feet, hands, and eyes. To substitute books for them does not teach us to reason; it teaches us to use the reason of others rather than our own; it teaches us to believe much and to know little."

"Before you can get an art, you must first get your tools; and if you are to make good use of your tools, they must be fashioned sufficiently strong to stand use. To learn to think, we must accordingly exercise our limbs, our senses, and our bodily organs, for these are the tools of intellect. To get the best use of these tools, the body that supplies us with these tools must be kept strong and healthy. Not only is it a mistake that true reason is developed apart from the body, but it is a good bodily constitution that makes the workings of the mind easy and correct."

The passage shows how far Rousseau was from considering bodily development as a complete end in itself. It also indicates how far ahead he was of the psychology of his own day in his conception of the relation of the senses to knowledge. The current idea (and one that prevails too much even in our own time) was that the senses were a sort of gateway and avenue through which impressions traveled and then built up knowledge pictures of the world. Rousseau saw that they are a part of the apparatus of action by which we adjust ourselves to our environment, and that instead of being passive receptacles they are directly connected with motor activities—with the use of hands and legs. In this respect he was more advanced than some of his successors who emphasized the importance of sense contact with objects, for the latter thought of the senses simply as purveyors of information about objects instead of instruments of the necessary adjustments of human beings to the world around them.

Consequently, while he makes much of the senses and suggests many games for cultivating them, he never makes the mere training of the senses an object on its own account. "It is not enough," he says, "to use the senses in order to train them; we must learn to judge by their means—we cannot really see, hear, or touch except as we have learned. A merely mechanical use of the senses may strengthen the body without improving the judgment. It is all very well to swim, run, jump, whip a top, throw stones. But we have eyes and ears as well as arms and legs, and these organs are necessary for learning the use of the rest. Do not, then, merely exercise strength, but exercise the senses as the powers by which strength is guided. Make the best use of every one of them, and check the results of one by another. Measure, count, weigh, compare. Do not use force till you have estimated the resistance; let estimation of the effect always precede application of the means. Get the child interested in avoiding superfluous and insufficient efforts. If you train him to calculate the consequences of what he does and then to correct the errors of his prevision by experience, the more he does, the wiser he will become.''

One more contrast between teaching which guides natural growth and teaching which imposes adult accomplishments should be noticed. The latter method puts a premium upon accumulating information in the form of symbols. Quantity rather than quality of knowledge is emphasized; results that may be exhibited when asked for rather than personal attitude and method are demanded. Development emphasizes the need of intimate and extensive personal acquaintance with a small number of typical situations with a view to mastering the way of dealing with the problems of experience, not the piling up of information. As Rousseau points out, the facility with which children lend themselves to our false methods is a constant source of deception to us. We know—or fancy we know—what statements mean, and so when the child uses the proper form of words, we attribute the same understanding to him. "The apparent ease with which children learn is their ruin. We fail to see that this very ease proves that they are not learning. Their shining, polished brain merely reflects, as in a mirror, the things we show them." Rousseau describes in a phrase the defect of teaching *about* things instead of bringing to pass an acquaintance with the relations of the things themselves. "You think you are teaching him what the world is like; he is only learning the map." Extend the illustration from geography to the whole wide realm of knowledge, and you have the gist of much of our teaching from the elementary school through the college.

Rousseau has the opposite method in mind when he says, "Among the many short cuts to science we badly need one to teach us the art of learning with difficulty." Of course his idea is not to make things difficult for the sake of having them difficult, but to avoid the simulation of learning found in repeating the formulæ of learning, and to substitute for it the slow and sure process of personal discovery. Textbooks and lectures give the results of other

To learn to think, we must exercise our limbs. (Francis Parker School, Chicago.)

EDUCATION AS DEVELOPMENT

men's discoveries, and thus seem to provide a short cut to knowledge; but the outcome is just a meaningless reflecting back of symbols with no understanding of the facts themselves. The further result is mental confusion; the pupil loses his original mental sure-footedness; his sense of reality is undermined. "The first meaningless phrase, the first thing taken for granted on the authority of another without the pupil's seeing its meaning for himself, is the beginning of the ruin of judgment." And again: "What would you have him think about, when you do all the thinking for him?" (And we must not forget that the organized material of our texts and set lessons represents the thinking of others.) "You then complete the task of discrediting reason in his mind by making him use such reason as he has upon the things which seem of the least use to him."

If it was true in Rousseau's day that information, knowledge, as an end in itself, is an "unfathomable and shoreless ocean," it is much more certain that the increase of science since his day has made absurd the identification of education with the mere accumulation of knowledge. The frequent criticism of existing education on the ground that it gives a smattering and superficial impression of a large and miscellaneous number of subjects, is just. But the desired remedy will not be found in a return to mechanical and meager teaching of the three R's, but rather in a surrender of our feverish desire to lay out the whole field of knowledge into various studies, in order to "cover the ground." We must substitute for this futile and harmful aim the better ideal of dealing thoroughly with a small number of typical experiences in such a way as to master the tools of learning, and present situations that make pupils hungry to acquire additional knowledge. By the conventional method of teaching, the pupil learns maps instead of the world—the symbol instead of the fact. What the pupil really needs is not exact information about topography, but how to find out for himself. "See what a difference there is between the knowledge of your pupils and the ignorance of mine. They learn maps; he makes them." *To find out how to make knowledge when it is needed* is the true end of the acquisition of information in school, not the information itself.

CHAPTER II

AN EXPERIMENT IN EDUCATION AS NATURAL DEVELOPMENT

Rousseau's teaching that education is a process of natural growth has influenced most theorizing upon education since his time. It has influenced the practical details of school work to a less degree. Occasionally, however, experimenters have based their plans upon his principles. Among these experiments is one conducted by Mrs. Johnson at Fairhope, Alabama. To this spot during the past few years students and experts have made pilgrimages, and the influence of Mrs. Johnson's model has led to the starting of similar schools in different parts of the United States. Mrs. Johnson carries on a summer course for training teachers by giving a working object lesson in her ideas at Greenwich, Connecticut, where a school for children has been conducted as a model.

Her main underlying principle is Rousseau's central idea; namely: The child is best prepared for life as an adult by experiencing in childhood what has meaning to him as a child; and, further, the child has a right to enjoy his childhood. Because he is a growing animal who must develop so as to live successfully in the grown-up world, nothing should be done to interfere with growth, and everything should be done to further the full and free development of his body and his mind. These two developments go on together; they are inseparable processes and must both be constantly borne in mind as of equal importance.

Mrs. Johnson criticizes the conventional school of to-day. She says it is arranged to make things easy for the teacher who wishes quick and tangible results; that it disregards the full development of the pupils. It is arranged on the fatal plan of a hothouse, forcing to a sterile show, rather than fostering all-around growth. It does not foster an individuality capable of an enduring resistance and of creative activities. It disregards the *present* needs of the child; the fact that he is living a full life each year and hour, not waiting to live in some period defined by his elders, when school is a thing of the past. The distaste of children for school is a natural and necessary result of such mistakes as these. Nature has not adapted the young animal to the narrow desk,

AN EXPERIMENT

the crowded curriculum, the silent absorption of complicated facts. His very life and growth depend upon motion, yet the school forces him into a cramped position for hours at a time, so that the teacher may be sure he is listening or studying books. Short periods of exercise are allowed as a bribe to keep him quiet the rest of the time, but these relaxations do not compensate for the efforts which he must make. The child is eager to move both mentally and physically. Just as the physical growth must progress together with the mental, so it is in the separate acts of a child. His bodily movements and his mental awakening are mutually dependent upon each other.

It is not enough to state this principle without carrying its proof into practice, says Mrs. Johnson. The child with the well-nourished, active body is the child who is most anxious to do and to know things. The need of activity must be met in the exercise of the school, hour by hour; the child must be allowed to move about both in work and in play, to imitate and to discover for himself. The world of objects around him is an unexplored hemisphere to the child even at the age of six years, a world constantly enlarging to his small vision as his activities carry him further and further in his investigations, a world by no means so commonplace to him as to the adult. Therefore, let the child, while his muscles are soft and his mind susceptible, look for himself at the world of things both natural and artificial, which is for him the source of knowledge.

Instead of providing this chance for growth and discovery, the ordinary school impresses the little one into a narrow area, into a melancholy silence, into a forced attitude of mind and body, till his curiosity is dulled into surprise at the strange things happening to him. Very soon his body is tired of his task and he begins to find ways of evading his teacher, to look about him for an escape from his little prison. This means that he becomes restless and impatient, in the language of the school, that he loses interest in the small tasks set for him and consequently in that new world so alluring a little while ago. The disease of indifference has attacked his sensitive soul, before he is fairly started on the road to knowledge.

The reason for having a school where children work together is that the child must learn to work with others. Granting this, Mrs. Johnson has tried to find a plan giving the utmost liberty of individual development. Because the young child is unfitted by reason of his soft

AN EXPERIMENT

muscles and his immature senses to the hard task of settling down to fine work on the details of things, he should not begin school life by learning to read and write, nor by learning to handle small playthings or tools. He must continue the natural course he began at home of running from one interesting object to another, of inquiring into the meaning of these objects, and above all of tracing the relation between the different objects. All this must be done in a large way so that he gets the names and bearings of the obvious facts as they appear in their order. Thus the obscure and difficult facts come to light one after another without being forced upon the child's attention by the teacher. One discovery leads to another, and the interest of pursuit leads the child of his own accord into investigations that often amount to severe intellectual discipline.

Following this path of natural growth, the child is led into reading, writing, arithmetic, geography, etc., by his own desire to know. We must wait for the desire of the child, for the consciousness of need, says Mrs. Johnson; then we must promptly supply the means to satisfy the child's desire. Therefore, the age of learning to read is put off until the child is well grounded in his experience and knowledge of the larger relations of things. Mrs. Johnson goes so far as to prevent children from learning to read at too early an age. At eight or nine years, she thinks they are keen to explore books just as they have previously explored things. By this time they recognize the need and use of the information contained in books; they have found out they can get this information in no other way. Hence, the actual learning to read is hardly a problem; children teach themselves. Under the stimulus of interest in arriving at the knowledge of some particular subject, they overcome the mechanical difficulty of reading with ease and rapidity. Reading is not to them an isolated exercise; it is a means of acquiring a much-desired object. Like climbing the pantry shelves, its difficulties and dangers are lost sight of in the absorbing desire to satisfy the mental appetite.

Each of the subjects of the curriculum should be given to the child to meet a demand on his part for a greater knowledge of relations than he can get from studying objects. Arithmetic and abstract notions represented by figures are meaningless to the child of six, but numbers as a part of the things he is playing with or using every day are so full of meaning that he soon finds he cannot get along without a knowledge of them.

Mrs. Johnson is trying an experiment under conditions which hold in public schools, and she believes that her methods are feasible for any public school system. She charges practically no tuition, and any child is welcome. She calls her methods of education "organic" because they follow the natural growth of the pupil. The school aims to provide for the child the occupations and activities necessary at each stage of development for his unfolding at that stage. Therefore, she insists that general development instead of the amount of information acquired, shall control the classification of the pupils. Division into groups is made where it is found that the children naturally divide themselves. These groups are called "Life Classes" instead of grades. The first life class ends between the eighth and ninth years; the second between the eleventh and twelfth, and since an even more marked change of interests and tastes occurs at the period of adolescence, there are distinct high-school classes. The work within the group is then arranged to give the pupils the experiences which are needed at that age for the development of their bodies, minds, and spirits.

Doing forced tasks, assignment of lessons to study, and ordinary examinations have no share in the Fairhope curriculum. Hence, the children do not acquire that dislike of learning and mistrust of what a teacher or text-book says, which are unfortunately so common among scholars in the ordinary school. They exercise their instincts to learn naturally, without that self-consciousness which comes from having been forced to keep their minds on examinations and promotions.

Bright and intelligent children often acquire a distaste for the schoolroom and what comes out of it, which they not only never wholly outgrow but which is a real handicap to them as they grow up, often preventing them from taking their college work seriously, and making them suspicious of all ideas not actually deduced from their own experience outside the classroom. Perhaps they grow so docile they acquiesce in all authoritative statements whatsoever, and lose their sense of reality. We tell our children that books are the storehouses of the world, and that they contain the heritage of the past without which we would be savages; then we teach them so that they hate books of information and discount what a teacher tells them. Incompetency is general not because

AN EXPERIMENT

people are not instructed enough as children, but because they cannot and do not make any use of what they learn. The extent to which this is due to an early mistrust of school and the learning associated with it cannot be overstated.

The students at Fairhope will never have this handicap to contend with. They are uniformly happy in school, and enthusiastically proclaim their "love" for it. Not only is the work interesting to the group as a whole, but no individual child is forced to a task that does not appeal; each pupil may do as he pleases as long as he does not interfere with any one else. The children are not freed, however, from all discipline. They must keep at work while they are in school, and learn not to bother their neighbors, as well as to help them when necessary. Caprice or laziness does not excuse a child from following a healthy or useful régime.

Mrs. Johnson feels that children in their early years are neither moral nor immoral, but simply unmoral; their sense of right and wrong has not yet begun to develop. Therefore, they should be allowed as much freedom as possible; prohibitions and commands, the result of which either upon themselves or their companions they cannot understand, are bound to be meaningless; their tendency is to make the child secretive and deceitful. Give a child plenty of healthy activity. When he must be disciplined, do not appeal to a sense which he has not got, but show him by a little pain if necessary what his naughty act meant to his playmate. If he is to share in fun and good things with his family and friends, he must behave so that they will want his company. This is a motive which, a young child can understand, for he knows when his friends are agreeable or disagreeable to him. There is less in such a scheme of discipline that impels the child to shirk or conceal, to lie or to become too conscious of his acts, than in a discipline based on moral grounds, which seems to the child to be a mere excuse for forcing him to do something simply because some grown person wants it done.

Lack of self-consciousness is a positive gain on the side of happiness. Mrs. Johnson's scheme of discipline contributes toward that love of school and work which all teaching aims to establish. When work is interesting, it is not necessary to hamper children in their performance of it by meaningless restrictions and petty prohibitions. When children work willingly they come to associate learning with the doing of what is congenial. This is undoubtedly of positive moral value. It helps develop a confident, cheerful attitude toward work; an ability to face a task without dislike or repulsion, which is of more real value in character building than doing hard, distasteful tasks, or forcing attention and obedience.

The division into age groups or "life classes" takes away that emphasis upon the pupils' failures and shortcomings which is bound to be more or less evident where pupils are graded according to their proficiency in books. The child who is slow mentally is not made to feel that he is disgraced. Attention is not called to him and he is not prodded, scolded, or "flunked." Unaware of his own weaknesses, he retains the moral support of confidence in himself; and his hand work and physical accomplishments frequently give him prestige among his fellows. Mrs. Johnson believes that the recitations and examination of the ordinary schoolroom are merely devices to make the work easier for the teacher; while the consciousness of what he does or does not "know," resulting from marks and grades, is harmful to the child just as an emphasis of his failures is harmful.

Especially marked is the contrast of the classroom exercises at Fairhope with recitations where, sitting still with their books closed, the children are subject to a fire of questions from the teacher to find out how much they remember of a lesson they are supposed to have "studied" alone. To quote again from Rousseau: "He (the teacher) makes a point of showing that no time has been wasted; he provides his pupils with goods that can be readily displayed in the shop windows, accomplishments which can be shown off at will. . . . If the child is to be examined, he is set to display his wares; he spreads them out; satisfies those who behold them, packs up his bundle, and goes his way. Too many questions are tedious and revolting to most of us and especially to children. After a few minutes their attention flags; they cease to listen to your everlasting questions and they answer at random." At Fairhope the children do the work, and the teacher is there to help them to know, not to have them give back what they have memorized. Tests are often conducted with books open, since they are not to show the teacher what the child can remember, but rather to discover his progress in ability to use books. Lessons are not assigned, but the books are open in the hands of the pupils and with the teacher they discuss the text, getting out of it all the joy and information possible. This stimulates a real love of books, so that these children who have never been as-

AN EXPERIMENT

signed a lesson to study, voluntarily study the text after the class work. They are not tempted to cheat, for they are not put in the position of having to show off.

The result of this system of discipline and study over and above satisfactory progress in the "three R's," is freedom from self-consciousness on the mental and moral side; the ability of a child to put all his native initiative and enthusiasm into his work; the power to indulge his natural desire to learn; thus preserving joy in life and a confidence in himself which liberates all his energies for his work. He likes school and forgets that he is "learning"; for learning comes unconsciously as a by-product of experiences which he recognizes as worth while on their own account.

The following activities have been worked out at Fairhope as a substitute for the usual curriculum: physical exercise, nature study, music, hand work, field geography, story telling, sense culture, fundamental conceptions of number, dramatizations, and games. In the second class map drawing and descriptive geography are added, for reading is acquired, and the number work is modified by the knowledge of figures. Each lesson is planned as a concrete experience with a definite end in view, appealing to the child as desirable. As would be expected from the emphasis put upon following the development of the child, physical exercise plays an important part in the day's work. It comes every day, during the regular school hours and usually in the first part of the morning while the children are fresh and energetic. For an hour the school is outdoors in a field the children call "the gym." Bars, horses, etc., are scattered about, and there is some one there to help them try new things and see that the work is well balanced, but formal gymnastics in the accepted meaning of the term do not exist. Mrs. Johnson believes that the distaste of children is sufficient reason for doing away with them, and that, since the growing child is constantly seeking of his own accord opportunities to stretch and exercise his muscles, all the school needs to do is to supply the opportunity, seeing to it that this is not indulged to the point of harming the child. The children fall naturally into groups; those who want to swing on the bars and rings, those who want to climb, to jump, or run, or throw, etc. Running usually takes the form of races; a tree is used as a target in the stone throwing contests. The children themselves have invented games to use on the apparatus, and the hour in

(1) An hour a day spent in the "Gym."
(2) The Gully is a favorite textbook.
    (Fairhope, Ala.)

AN EXPERIMENT

the "gym" is one of the busiest in the day. It leaves the children eager and stimulated for their mental work, since it has meant no overworking of one set of muscles, no dull repetition of meaningless movements at some one else's command. Besides this regular time for exercise, the children may study outdoors, and many of the classes are conducted in the open air. Indoors there are games, handwork, and dramatizations, all of which contribute to the physical well-being of the children. There are no cramping desks, the pupil may sit where or how he pleases, or even move from place to place if he does not disturb his fellows. The classes go on in a room in which two groups, each of fifteen or more children, are working, and the necessary quiet and order exist.

Nature study and field geography are conducted almost entirely out of doors. The children go into the fields and woods and look at the trees and flowers, ask questions about them, examine the differences in bark, leaves, and flowers, tell each other what they think, and use their books to answer questions that the trees and plants have suggested to them. They learn the meaning of the words pistils, stamens, and petals with flowers they have gathered, or watch a bee carrying pollen from plant to plant.

Individual pupils are encouraged to tell the class what they may have learned at home, to bring flowers from their gardens, or to tell of things they have seen. The class visit a neighboring truck farm, recognize as many vegetables as they can, and learn the names and characteristics of the new ones. When they are back in the schoolroom those that can write make a list of all the vegetables they can remember, thus combining with their nature lesson a lesson in writing. There is a garden in the school grounds where the pupils learn to plow, rake, and plant, watch their seeds come up and grow and flower. In a little plot of ground that is their own, they observe all the phases in the cycle of plant life, and besides get the benefits of the moral training that comes from carrying through a piece of work that lasts several months and demands constant thought and care. This sort of work plays a large part in the curriculum of the younger children, for it seems to belong particularly to their world; to the world of definite concrete objects which they see about them every day, which they can handle and play with, and which consequently arouse their curiosity.

The field geography is conducted in much the same way. Even the very young children acquire a good idea of the different sorts of rock formations, of the action of the wind and rain, of river currents, by direct observation; if text-books are used they come afterwards, to explain or amplify something the pupils have seen. The soil about the school is clay and after a rain the smallest stream furnishes excellent examples of the ways of rivers, erosions, watersheds, floods, or changing currents, while an explanation of tides or the Gulf Stream is made vital by a little trip to the Bay. A gully near the school building not only furnishes a splendid place for play but serves as a text-book in mountain ranges, valleys, and soil and rock formation. All this serves as an excellent foundation and illustration for the descriptive geography which comes later. The more advanced geography is principally commercial geography; and with the scientific background that the pupils have already obtained, the real significance of the relations between climates and crops, industries, exports and imports, and social conditions is much more likely to be understood.

The value of handwork is strongly emphasized at Fairhope, consistently with the emphasis put on physical growth. The little child must go on learning to coördinate with more and more skill his muscular movements if his body is to be developed to the highest standards of health and efficiency, and nothing contributes to this better than the controlled and rather delicate motions necessary for making things with the hands. The fact that he is making things gives just the stimulus the child needs to enable him to keep on at the task, to repeat over and over the same efforts of mind, hand, and eye, to give him real control of himself in the process. The benefits of handwork on the utilitarian side are just as great. The child learns how to use the ordinary tools of life, the scissors, knife, needle, plane, and saw, and gets an appreciation of the artists' tools, paint and clays, which lasts the rest of his life. If he is a child with initiative and inventiveness he finds a natural and pleasant outlet for his energies. If he is dreamy or unpractical, he learns a respect for manual work, and gains something toward becoming a well-rounded human being. Boys and girls alike do cooking and carpentry work, for the object of the work is not to train them for any trade or profession, but to train them to be capable, happy members of society. Painting or clay modeling play quite as large a rôle, even with the little ones, as carpentry or sewing, providing they serve a purpose or are

AN EXPERIMENT 35

sufficiently connected with other work to hold the pupil's interest. A sense of the beautiful is not consciously present in small children and must be developed through their handling of every-day objects if it is to become a real force in their lives. Therefore "art" is taught as part of the handwork, the story telling, the dramatization, or the nature study. The youngest children in clay modeling, painting, weaving paper mats, making paper or wooden toys, etc., are asked as much as possible to suggest things they want to make. With the acquisition of skill, they go on making more and more difficult objects; pupils of nine or ten make raffia baskets, boats, and dolls' furniture.

The story telling and dramatization are very closely connected and (up to the age of about ten) take the place of the usual bookwork. Stories of literary value, suited in subject matter to the age of the pupils, are told or read to them, and they in turn are asked to tell stories they have heard outside of school. After the ninth or tenth year, when the children have learned to read, they read stories from books, either to themselves or aloud, and then the whole class discuss them. The Greek myths, the Iliad, and the Odyssey are favorites at this age, and very frequently without directions from the teacher, a class will act out a whole story, such as the Fall of Troy, or any tale that has appealed especially to their dramatic imagination. The school believes that this is the true way for young people to approach literature, if they are to learn to love and appreciate it, not simply to study the text for strange words and figures of speech. The pupils are not allowed to use books until the eighth or ninth year, and by this time they have realized so keenly their need, they beg for help in learning. The long, tiresome drill necessary for six-year-old children is eliminated. Each child is anxious to read some particular book, so there is little or no need to trap his attention, or to insist on an endless repetition. Mrs. Johnson believes also that it is better for the natural physical and mental development of the child, if learning to write and figure is put off as late as possible. Then pupils approach it with a consciousness of their real need for it, of the help it will be to them in their daily life. Their background of knowledge of things and skill acquired through handwork renders the actual processes of learning comparatively simple. Mrs. Johnson is convinced that a child who does not learn to read and write in her school until he is ten years old, is as well read

AN EXPERIMENT

at fourteen, and writes and spells as well as a child of fourteen in a school where the usual curriculum is followed.

The fundamental conception of number is taught orally. The smallest children begin by counting one another or the things about them. Then perhaps at the blackboard they will divide a line in half, then into three parts, then quarters. By means of objects or lines on the blackboard they next begin to add, to subtract, to take three-fourths, even to divide. The oral drill in this kind of work is constant, and the children become thoroughly familiar with the fundamental processes of arithmetic, before they can write a number or know the meaning of the addition or multiplication sign. Then when the time comes, at about the age of nine, to learn to write numbers, the drill is repeated by using the conventional signs instead of lines or objects. The school has found that this method does away with the usual struggles, especially in learning fractions and their handling. Long division and the other complicated processes are taught after the pupils can write well and easily, and no emphasis is put on formal analysis until repeated drill has made the children fairly familiar with, and proficient in, the process. Games and contests of all sorts invented by the individual teacher are used to make this drill interesting to the pupils.

Sense culture means the specific training of the child's body and muscles to respond accurately to the desire to perform definite muscular or other sense acts; or more technically it means motor-sensory coördination. Besides the general training coming from handwork and physical exercise, special games are arranged to exercise the different senses. The youngest class does relatively most of this sense gymnastic. The whole class sits motionless and in absolute silence; some child tiptoes from his seat to another part of the room, and then with his eyes shut every other child tries to tell where he is; or one child says something and the others try to guess who it was, by the voice. To train the sense of touch, a blindfolded child is given some ordinary objects, and by touching them tries to recognize them. One of the favorite games of the whole school was invented to train muscular accuracy. Children of different ages, divided into groups, throw stones at a large tree in the yard. This game has all the zest of competition, while teaching the eye and hand to work together, and exercising the whole body. The unusual physical control of the Fairhope pupils is seen best in the carpenter shop, where even the youngest children work and handle full-sized tools, hammers, saws, and planes and do not hurt themselves. There is a foot power jig-saw in the shop and it is an instructive sight to see a child of seven, too small to work the pedal, holding his piece of wood, turning and shaping it in the saw without hurting himself.

The Fairhope pupils compare favorably with pupils in the ordinary public schools. When for any reason they make a change, they have always been able to work with other children of their age without extra effort; they are apt to be stronger physically and are much more capable with their hands, while they have a real love of books and study that makes them equally strong on the purely cultural side of their work. The organic curriculum has been worked out in detail and in use longest for the younger children, but Mrs. Johnson is convinced the principle of her work will apply equally well to high school pupils and is beginning an experiment with high school children. Under her direction the school has proved a decided success. Time and larger opportunities will undoubtedly correct the weak spots and discrepancies that are bound to appear while any school is in the experimental stage. The school has provided conditions for wholesome, natural growth in small enough groups for the teacher (as a leader rather than an instructor) to become acquainted with the weaknesses of each child individually and then to adapt the work to the individual needs. It has demonstrated that it is possible for children to lead the same natural lives in school that they lead in good homes outside of school hours; to progress bodily, mentally, and morally in school without factitious pressure, rewards, examinations, grades, or promotions, while they acquire sufficient control of the conventional tools of learning and of study of books—reading, writing, and figuring—to be able to use them independently.

CHAPTER III

FOUR FACTORS IN NATURAL GROWTH

THE Elementary School of the University of Missouri, at Columbia, under the direction of Prof. J. L. Meriam, has much in common with Mrs. Johnson's school at Fairhope. In its fundamental idea, that education shall follow the natural development of the child, it is identical, but its actual organization and operation are sufficiently different to make a description of it suggestive. In common with most educational reformers, Professor Meriam believes the schools of the past have been too much concerned with teaching children adult facts. In attempting to systematize and standardize, the curriculum has ignored the needs of the individual child. He believes that the work and play of the school should be children's work and play; that the children should enjoy school. The life there should be like, only better than, the life of the children outside the school; better because they are helped to know how to play and work correctly and to do it with other children.

"Do children remember how they learned to talk? No, but their parents remember for them. Yet most of us, both children and adults, remember how we struggled in learning to read and write at school. We learned to talk simply by talking when we were in need or had something to say. We learned to say, 'Please, Mamma, give me a drink,' when we wanted a drink. We did not practice on such words at nine o'clock each morning. The pupils in the University Elementary School learn to read, to write, to draw, and to do other things, just when they need to do so. The pupils do in this school about what they would do at home, but they learn to do it better. They work and play. At home they are very active most of the time doing many things; and so they are in this school."

What would these children naturally be doing if there were no school? On the answer to this question Professor Meriam has based his curriculum, which contains but one subject that appears on the ordinary program; namely, handwork. They would, he says, be playing outdoors, exercising their bodies by running, jumping, or throwing; they would be talking together in groups, discussing what they had seen or heard; they would be making things to use in their play: boats, bean bags, dolls, hammocks, or dresses; if they live in the country they would be watching animals or plants, making a garden or trying to fish. Every one recognizes that the child develops quite as much through such activities as through what he learns in school, and that what he learns out of school is much more apt to become a part of his working knowledge, because it is entirely pleasurable and he recognizes the immediate use of it. Again, these occupations are all closely connected with the business of living; and we send our children to school to learn this. What, then, could be more natural than making the school's curriculum of such material? This is what Professor Meriam does. The day is divided into four periods, which are devoted to the following elements: play, stories, observation, and handwork. For the younger children the work is drawn almost entirely from the community in which they live; they spend their time finding out more about the things they are already familiar with. As they grow older their interest naturally reaches out to remoter things and to the processes and reasons back of things; and they begin to study history, geography, and science.

The time of the first three grades is divided

in this way: From 9 to 10:30, observation; 10:30 to 11, physical exercises; from 11 to 12, play; 1:30 to 3, stories; and 3 to 4, handwork.

The observation period is devoted to the study of one topic, and this topic may take only a single morning or it may take several weeks. While there is a general plan for the year's work, if the children bring up anything which seems of importance to them and which fits in, the program is laid aside and the teacher helps the pupils in their study of their own problem. This might be true of any of the studies of the day; the program is flexible, the school aims to meet the individual needs of the child and the group. The observation periods of the first three grades are devoted to a study of flowers, trees, and fruits; birds and animals, of the weather and the changing seasons, of holidays, of the town grocery store, or the neighborhood dwellings, and the clothing that the children see for sale in the stores. The pupils learn to read and write and figure only as they feel the need of it to enlarge their work. The nature work is taught as much as possible out of doors; the children take walks with the teacher and talk about the trees, plants, and animals they meet on their way; they gather tadpoles and fish for the school aquarium and pick out a tree to watch

Games often require muscular skill, reading, writing, and arithmetic. (University School, Columbia, Mo.)

FOUR FACTORS 45

and keep a record of for the whole year. Their study of the weather also lasts through the whole year; they watch the changing seasons, what things look like in the fall and what happens as winter begins, what the plants and animals do in winter, etc. In this way they watch the whole cycle of the year, and learn unconsciously the relation between their own climate and the vegetation and animal life about them.

The study of their own food, shelter, and clothing is concentrated into a consecutive period, and as interest and time dictate it is added to by a study of some phases of local life that are not concerned with the actual necessities of life. They learn about their neighbors' recreations and pleasures by studying the jewelry store and the circus, or the community interests of their parents by studying the local fire department and post-office.

The method of study is the same for all work. First, with help from the teacher the children tell all they know about the subject they are beginning to study; if it is food, each child has an opportunity to say anything he can think of about it; what his own family eats, where the food comes from, how it is taken care of, what he has noticed in the grocery stores, etc. Then the whole class with the teacher make a visit to the grocery store, spend perhaps all the morning there, each child trying to see how much he can find out for himself. Before they start the teacher has called their attention to the fact that the things are sold by the quart, etc., for the subject of weights and measures seems to be of absorbing interest to the children when approached from this side. Some first grade children have proved to be remarkably keen detectives in noticing the grocer's innumerable devices for making quantities look greater than they are. The pupils are also encouraged to note and compare prices, and to bring food budgets from home whenever their parents are willing. When they return to their classroom they again discuss what they have seen, and those who can write make a list with prices of all the articles which they can remember, or write an account of their visit, which is dictated by the teacher from the oral accounts the children themselves have given of it.

The pupils who cannot read will draw a picture of the grocery store or perhaps have a reading lesson in the catalogue the grocer has given them. Later they will study the way the grocer delivers his goods to his patrons, and in a very general way where the things come from. They will bring grocers' bills from home, compare them, add them up, and discuss the question of economical and nutritious food. Perhaps they will do the same thing with the milk and bakery business, before moving on to the question of the houses in the neighborhood. This and the clothing and recreation of the town will be studied in the same way. Later the class will visit the fire department and the post-office and find out what each is for and how they are conducted. This and the study of local amusements usually come in the third grade. The opportunity for the constant use of reading, writing, and arithmetic, and for drill in the correct use of spoken English, is obvious. Professor Meriam is insistent upon the fact that this study of the community in which the child lives is made for the educational value of the work itself to the pupil, never as a mere cloak for the teaching of "the three R's," which must be done only as it contributes directly to the work the children are doing.

The period devoted to games by the first three grades is of the same educational value. The children are exercising their bodies, learning to control them and to make skillful motions aimed at some immediate result. Much variety and liberty is allowed in this work, and the teacher is only an observer. Most of the games the children play are competitive, for they have found that the element of skill and chance is what the pupils need to make them work hard at the games. Bean bags and nine pins are favorites; any game, in fact, where they can keep score; the teacher acts as scorekeeper for the little children, and when the game is over they copy the score in a folder to refer to and see how they progress. The better they play, the more they enjoy the game; so they watch the best player, studying how he moves and stands, and make drawings. The teacher also writes on the board some of the things the pupils say as they play, and at the end of the game they find a reading lesson which they have made themselves and which gives an account of their game; in copying this into their folders they have a writing lesson. The children are allowed to talk and laugh as much as they please while they are playing, and this is an English lesson. Great variety is introduced into the games so as to encourage the pupils to talk freely, and added stimulus is given by using interesting things to play with, bright colored balls, dolls, and gaily painted "roly-polys." The new words and phrases the children use are written down in the daily account of the game, and in this way their vocabulary is enlarged in a natural way.

The hour devoted to stories is no more a reading and writing lesson than all the rest of the day's work. Children immensely enjoy good stories, therefore they ought to be given plenty of opportunity to become acquainted with them. During this period, the teacher and the children tell stories to each other; not stories they have studied from their primers, but stories that they already know, that they have listened to, or read because they enjoyed them. Every child likes to be listened to, and they soon discover they must tell their story well or they will get no audience. Some stories they tell by acting them out, others by drawing. Soon they want to learn a new group of stories, and then, quite naturally, they go to the school library, pick out a story book and read. It has been found that the first grade pupils read from twelve to thirty books during the year; the second grade pupils from twenty-five to fifty. In this way they learn to read, to read good books—for there is nothing else in the library—and to read them well, for they always have the desire to find a story to tell to their class, or one that they can act. Appreciation of good literature begins very early in this way, or rather, it is never lost. Very small children always enjoy most the best stories—Mother Goose, Hans Andersen, or Kipling's "Just So Stories." The dislike of books gained in school turns children from literature to trash. But if children are allowed and encouraged to hear, and read, and act out these stories in school just as they would at home—that is, for the sake of the fun there is in it—they will keep their good taste and enjoyment of good books. Songs, says Professor Meriam, are another sort of story, and little children sing for the fun of it, for the story of the song; so the singing at this school is part of the story work, and the children work and learn to sing better, in order to increase their enjoyment.

Children are always clamoring to "make something." Professor Meriam takes this fact as sufficient grounds for making handwork a regular part of the curriculum and having it occupy an hour a day, a period which usually seems so short to the pupils that they take their work home. The youngest children, boys and girls alike, go into the carpenter shop and learn to handle tools and to make things: furniture for their dolls, a boat, or some present to take home. Weaving and sewing interest both boys and girls alike and give scope to the young child for beauty and utility, so they do a lot of it. The youngest begin usually with dolls' hammocks; then they learn to do coarse cross-stitching and crocheting. An entire class, especially among the youngest children, usually make the same thing at the same time, but they may suggest what they want to make, and the older children are allowed a great deal of liberty. The work naturally increases in variety and complexity as the pupils grow older, and as they acquire skill in the handling of tools. Some of the fifth and sixth grade boys have made excellent pieces of furniture which are in constant use in the school. The handwork furnishes another opportunity for drawing and color work, in the making of drawings for patterns.

With the fourth grade there is a marked shift in the work, due to the widening interests that are coming to the child. The day is divided then into three periods, which are devoted to industries, stories, and handwork. Organized games no longer appeal to the pupils; they want their play outdoors, or in the freedom of a big gymnasium, where they can play rougher, noisier games, and they are big enough to keep their own scores in their heads. The "industries" period takes the place of the "observation'' of the younger children, and continues the same sort of work. The child has learned the meaning of the immediate objects he sees about him, their relation to himself and his friends, and he is ready to go on and enlarge this knowledge so as to take in the things he cannot see, processes and reasons, and relations that embrace the whole community, or more communities, and finally the whole world.

In the same way that the younger children study their immediate environment, the fourth grade studies the industries that go on in their own neighborhood: the shoe factory, the flour mill, the work in the wheat and corn fields. They go on excursions to the factory and farm, and their work in the classroom is based on what they see on their trips. Their writing and composition are the stories of their trips, which they write; their reading, the books that tell about farming or shoemaking; their arithmetic the practical problems they find the farmer or foreman doing; all done so that it will contribute to the pupils' understanding of the industry he is studying. Geography too comes from these trips. It answers the questions: Why do they grow wheat? Where will it grow best in the neighborhood and why? etc. This school happens to be situated in a small town where the industries are chiefly agricultural, but obviously such a plan could easily be adapted to any community by substituting the industries that are found in the immediate neighborhood.

In the fifth and sixth years the study of industries is continued, but the scope is extended to include the principal industries of the world. Here, of course, pupils must learn to substitute more and more the printed page for their former excursions. This includes drill in reading, writing, and mathematics, related to earlier studies, and also more and more geography. The use of the library becomes of great importance, for the pupils are not given one text-book from which they study and recite. Work in geography begins with this question: What becomes of the things made in this town, which we do not use up? The next step is: Where else are these same things made, and are they made in the same way? What else is made in that place and how is it done? Then, where and how are the things made that we get from elsewhere? No one text-book could suffice for this work, and if it did it would contradict the idea of the school that the children should learn by investigation. They must find for themselves from among the books in the library the ones that tell about the particular industry they are studying. Every child does not read the same book, and as far as possible each pupil makes some contribution to the discussion. Just as in the lower grades, the older pupils all make folders where they keep their descriptions of the industries and illustrations of machines and processes.

In the seventh and highest grade in the school, the study of industries is continued as history; that is, the history of the industries connected with clothing, feeding, and housing is taken up. The pupils study the history of shelter from the first beginnings with a cave or a brush thicket, through the tents of the wandering tribes and the Greek and Roman house, to the steel skyscraper of to-day. They study the history of agriculture and learn to understand the development of the steam reaper and thresher from the wooden stick of the savage. The study of the industries in these four higher grades includes a study of the institutions of government. The fourth grade studies the local post-office, in the fifth and sixth they study the mail system of the United States, and then how letters are carried to all parts of the world. The seventh grade studies the history of some of these institutions. Part of their time during the past year was devoted to finding out how the different peoples of the world have fought their battles and organized their armies, first by means of reading and then by discussing what they had read. Each pupil kept a record of this work, writing a short paper on the army of each country he studied and illustrating it as he cared to.

The story period of the four highest grades continues the work begun in the lower grades. Music and art become more and more concentrated into it. The children continue reading and discussing what they have read. Each pupil keeps a record of the books he reads with a short account of the story and reasons why he liked it, and these records are kept on a shelf in the library where any other pupil can consult them for help in his choice of books. Even in high school, Professor Meriam does not believe in teaching composition for its own sake, nor literature by the usual method of analysis. All the work of the school is a constant drill in English, and by helping the pupils to use and write good English during every school hour, more is accomplished than by concentrating the work into one hour of formal drill.

The teaching of French and German is also considered part of story work. It is a study the pupils take for the pleasure they get from talking and reading another language; for the sake of the literature they will be able to read. For this reason it finds its place in the curriculum among the things that are purely cultural: for recreation and pleasure. The studies that come under the title of "stories" are the only ones where homework is given. The children come to school to do their work, and it is not fair to ask them to do this same work at home as well. They should look forward to school as a pleasure, if they are to get the utmost benefit out of it, but if the doing of set tasks becomes associated with school work, the pupil's interest in his work in school is bound to diminish. If, however, some of the school work is regarded as appropriate to leisure and recreation, it is natural that the children should keep on with it out of school hours, in their homes.

The school has been working with this program for eight years, and has about 120 pupils. The school building has few rooms and these are connected with large folding doors. At least two and usually three grades work in the same room, and the pupils are allowed freedom to move about and talk to each other as long as they do not disturb their classmates.

One teacher takes charge of an entire room, about thirty-five children, divided into several groups, each doing a different thing. Individual teachers in some of the neighboring country public schools have also followed the program through one grade and have found that the pupils were all ready for promotion at the end of the year and that they did their work in the next grade with as much ease as if they had followed the usual formal drill. Records are being kept of the graduates of the elementary school. Most of them go into the high school of the university, where there is every opportunity to watch them closely. They find no unusual difficulty in keeping up with the regular college preparatory work, and their marks and the age at which they enter college indicate that their elementary training has given them some advantages over the public school pupils in ability to do the hard formal studying.

Professor Meriam is also director of the high school, but has not as yet changed the regular college preparatory curriculum, except in the English. He expects to do so, however, and believes an equally radical reorganization of the work will have beneficial results. In the high school, English is not taught at all as a separate study, but work on it is continued along the same lines followed in the elementary school. A study of a certain number of graduates from the university schools and an equal number from the town high school, has indicated that the pupils who have received none of the usual training in English during their high school course do better work in their English courses in college than those who have followed the regular routine.

Of course, judging an educational experiment by the pupil's ability to "keep up" with the system the experiment is trying to improve, is of very little value. The purpose of the experiment is not to devise a method by which the teacher can teach more to the child in the same length of time, or even prepare him more pleasantly for his college course. It is rather to give the child an education which will make him a better, happier, more efficient human being, by showing him what his capabilities are and how he can exercise them, both materially and socially, in the world he finds about him. If, while a school is still learning how best to do this for its pupils, it can at the same time give them all they would have gained in a more conventional school, we can be sure there has been no loss. Any manual skill or bodily strength that their schooling has given

(1) **Printing teaches English.** (Francis Parker School, Chicago.)

(2) **The basis of the year's work.** (Indianapolis.)

them, or any enjoyment of the tasks of their daily life and the best that art and literature has to offer, are further definite gains that can be immediately seen and measured. All contribute to the larger aim, but the lives of all the pupils will furnish the only real test of the success or failure of any educational experiment that aims to help the whole of society by helping the whole individual.

CHAPTER IV

THE REORGANIZATION OF THE CURRICULUM

ROUSSEAU, while he was writing his Émile, was allowing his own children to grow up entirely neglected by their parents, abandoned in a foundling asylum. It is not strange then that his readers and students should center their interest in his theories, in his general contribution to education rather than in his account of the impractical methods he used to create that exemplary prig—Émile. If Rousseau himself had ever tried to educate any real children he would have found it necessary to crystallize his ideas into some more or less fixed program. In his anxiety to reach the ideal described in his theories, the emphasis of his interest would have unconsciously shifted to the methods by which he could achieve his ideal in the individual child. The child should spend his time on things that are suited to his age. The teacher immediately asks what these things are? The child should have an opportunity to develop naturally, mentally, spiritually, and physically.

How is the teacher to offer this opportunity and what does it consist in? Only in the very simplest environment where one teacher is working out her own theories is it possible to get along without a rather definite embodiment of the ideal in specific materials and methods. Therefore in reviewing some of the modern attempts at educational reform, we quite naturally find that emphasis has been put upon the curriculum.

Pestalozzi and Froebel were the two educators most zealous in reducing inspiration got from Rousseau into the details of schoolroom work. They took the vague idea of natural development and translated it into formulæ which teachers could use from day to day. Both were theorists, Froebel by temperament, Pestalozzi by necessity; but both made vigorous efforts to carry their theories into practice. They not only popularized the newer ideas about education, but influenced school practice more than any other modern educators. Pestalozzi substantially created the working methods of elementary education; while, as everybody knows, Froebel created a new kind of school, the kindergarten, for children too young to attend regular primary classes.

This combination of theoretical and practical

influence makes it important to discriminate between the points where they carried the idea of education as growth forward, and the points where, in their anxiety to supply a school program to be followed by everybody, they fell back upon mechanical and external methods. Personally, Pestalozzi was as heroic in life as Rousseau was the reverse. Devotion to others took with him the place occupied by a sentimental egotism in Rousseau. For this very reason, perhaps, he had a firm grasp on a truth which Rousseau never perceived. He realized that natural development for a man means a social development, since the individual's vital connections are with others even more than with nature. In his own words: "Nature educated man for social relations, and by means of social relations. Things are important in the education of man in proportion to the intimacies of social relations into which man enters." For this reason family life is the center of education, and, in a way, furnishes the model for every educational institution. In family life physical objects, tables, chairs, the trees in the orchard, the stones of the fence, have a social meaning. They are things which people use together and which influence their common actions.

Education in a medium where things have social uses is necessary for intellectual as well as for moral growth. The more closely and more directly the child learns by entering into social situations, the more genuine and effective is the knowledge he gains. Since power for dealing with remoter things comes from power gained in managing things close to us, "the direct sense of reality is formed only in narrow social circles, like those of family life. True human wisdom has for its bedrock an intimate knowledge of the immediate environment and trained capacity for dealing with it. The quality of mind thus engendered is simple and clear-sighted, formed by having to do with uncompromising realities and hence adapted to future situations. It is firm, sensitive and sure of itself."

"The opposite education is scattering and confused; it is superficial, hovering lightly over every form of knowledge, without putting any of it to use: a medley, wavering and uncertain." The moral is plain: Knowledge that is worthy of being called knowledge, training of the intellect that is sure to amount to anything, is obtained only by participating intimately and actively in activities of social life.

This is Pestalozzi's great positive contribution. It represents an insight gained in his own personal experience; for as an abstract thinker he was weak. It not only goes beyond Rousseau, but it puts what is true in Rousseau upon a sound basis. It is not, however, an idea that lends itself readily to formal statement or to methods which can be handed from one to another. Its significance is illustrated in his own early undertaking when he took twenty vagabond children into his own household and proceeded to teach them by means of farm pursuits in summer and cotton spinning and weaving in the winter, connecting, as far as possible, book instruction with these active occupations. It was illustrated, again later in his life, when he was given charge of a Swiss village, where the adults had been practically wiped out for resistance to an army of Napoleon. When a visitor once remarked: "Why, this is not a school; this is a household," Pestalozzi felt he had received his greatest compliment.

The other side of Pestalozzi is found in his more official school teaching career. Here also he attacked the purely verbal teaching of current elementary education and struggled to substitute a natural development. But instead of relying upon contact with objects used in active social pursuits (like those of the home), he fell back upon bare contact with the objects themselves. The result was a shift in Pestalozzi's fundamental idea. Presentation of objects by the teacher seemed to take the place of growth by means of personal activities. He was dimly conscious of the inconsistency, and tried to overcome it by saying that there are certain fixed laws of development which can be abstracted from the various experiences of particular human beings. Education cannot follow the development going on in individual children at a particular time; that would lead to confusion and chaos, anarchy and caprice. It must follow general laws derived from the individual cases.

At this point, the emphasis is taken from participation in social uses of things and goes over to dependence upon objects. In searching for general laws which can be abstracted from particular experiences, he found three constant things: geometrical form, number, and language—the latter referring, of course, not to isolated verbal expressions but to the statement of the qualities of things. In this phase of his activity as teacher, Pestalozzi was particularly zealous in building up schemes of object-lesson teaching in which children should learn the spatial and numerical relations of things and acquire a vocabulary for expressing all their qualities. The notion that object-lessons, by means of presentation of things to the senses, is the staple of elementary education thus came from Pestalozzi. Since it was concerned with external things and their presentation to the senses, this scheme of education lent itself to definite formulation of methods which could be passed on, almost mechanically, from one person to another.

In developing such methods, Pestalozzi hit upon the idea that the "order of nature" consists in going from the simple to the complex. It became his endeavor to find out in every subject the A B C (as he called it) of observation in that topic—the simplest elements that can be put before the senses. When these were mastered, the pupils were to pass on to various complications of these elements. Thus, in learning to read, children were to begin with combinations like A B, E B, I B, O B; then take up the reverse combinations B A, B E, B I, B O, etc., until having mastered all the elements, they could go on to complex syllables and finally to words and sentences. Number, music, drawing were all taught by starting with simple elements which could be put before the senses, and then proceeding to build up more complex forms in a graded order.

So great was the vogue of this procedure that the very word "method" was understood by many to signify this sort of analysis and combination of external impressions. To this day, it constitutes, with many people, a large part of what is understood by "pedagogy." Pestalozzi himself called it the psychologizing of teaching, and, more accurately, its mechanizing. He gives a good statement of his idea in the following words: "In the world of nature, imperfection in the bud means imperfect maturity. What is imperfect in its germ is crippled in its growth. In the development of its component parts, this is as true of the growth of the intellect as of an apple. We must, therefore, take care, in order to avoid confusion and superficiality in education, to make *first impressions of objects as correct and as complete as possible.* We must begin with the infant in the cradle, and take the training of the race out of the hands of blind sportive nature, and bring it under the power which the experience of the centuries has taught us to abstract from nature's own processes."

These sentences might be given a meaning to which no one could object. All of the educational reformers have rightly insisted upon the importance of the first years in which fundamental attitudes controlling later growth are fixed. There can be no doubt that if we could regulate the earlier relations of children to the world about them so that *all* ideas gained are certain, solid, definite, and right as far as they go, we might give children unconscious, intellectual standards which would operate later on with an efficacy quite foreign to our present experience. But the certainty and definiteness of geometrical forms, and of isolated qualities of objects are artificial. Correctness and completeness are gained at the expense of isolation from the every-day human experience of the child. It is possible for a child to learn the various properties of squares, rectangles, etc., and to acquire their names. But unless the squares and rectangles enter into his purposeful activities he is merely accumulating scholastic information. Undoubtedly it is better that the child should learn the names in association with the objects than to learn mere strings of words. But one is almost as far from real development as the other. Both are very far from the "firm, sensitive, and sure knowledge" which comes from using things for ends which appeal to the child. The things that the child uses in his household occupations, in gardening, in caring for animals, in his plays and games, have real simplicity and completeness of meaning for him. The simplicity of straight lines, angles, and quantities put before him just to be learned is mechanical and abstract.

For a long time the practical influence of Pestalozzi was confined to expelling from the schools reliance upon memorizing words that had no connection with things; to bringing object-lessons into the schools, and to breaking up every topic into its elements, or A B C, and then going on by graded steps. The failure of these methods to supply motives and to give real power made many teachers realize that things which the child has a use for are really simpler and more complete to him, even if he doesn't understand *everything* about them, than isolated elements. In the newer type of schools, there is a marked return (though of course quite independently of any reference to Pestalozzi) to his earlier and more vital idea of learning by taking a share in occupations and pursuits which are like those of daily life and which are engaged in by the friends about him.

Different schools have worked the matter out in different ways. In the Montessori schools there is still a good deal of effort to control the growth of mind by the material presented. In others, as in the Fairhope experiment, the material is incidental and informal, and the curriculum follows the direct needs of the pupils.

Most schools fall, of course, between these two currents. The child must develop, and naturally, but society has become so complicated, its demands upon the child are so important and continuous, that a great deal must be presented to him. Nature is a very extensive as well as compact thing in modern life, including not only the intricate material environment of the child, but social relations as well. If the child is to master these he must cover a great deal of ground. How is this to be done in the best way? Methods and materials must be used which are in themselves vital enough to represent to the child the whole of this compact nature which constitutes his world. The child and the curriculum are two operative forces, both of them developing and reacting on each other. In visiting schools the things that are interesting and helpful to the average school teacher are the methods, and the curriculum, the way the pupils spend their time; that is, the way the adjustment between the child and his environment is brought about.

"Learning by doing" is a slogan that might almost be offered as a general description of the way in which many teachers are trying to effect this adjustment. The hardest lesson a child has to learn is a practical one, and if he fails to learn it no amount of book knowledge will make up for it: it is this very problem of adjustment with his neighbors and his job. A practical method naturally suggests itself as the easiest and best way of solving this problem. On the face of it, the various studies—arithmetic, geography, language, botany, etc.—are in themselves experiences. They are the accumulation of the past of humanity, the result of its efforts and successes, for generation after generation. The ordinary school studies present this not as a mere accumulation, not as a miscellaneous heap of separate bits of experience, but in some organized way. Hence, the daily experiences of the child, his life from day to day, and the subject matter of the schoolroom, are parts of the same thing; they are the first and last steps in the life of a people. To oppose one to the other is to oppose the infancy and maturity of the same growing life; it is to set the moving tendency and the final result of the same power over against each other; it is to hold that the nature and the destiny of the child war with each other.

The studies represent the highest development possible in the child's simple every-day experiences. The task of the school is to take these crude experiences and organize them into science, geography, arithmetic, or whatever the lesson of the hour is. Since what the child already knows is part of some one subject that the teacher is trying to teach him, the method that will take advantage of this experience as a foundation stone on which to build the child's conscious knowledge of the subject appears as the normal and progressive way of teaching. And if we can enlarge the child's experience by methods which resemble as nearly as possible the ways that the child has acquired his beginning experiences, it is obvious that we have made a great gain in the effectiveness of our teaching. It is a commonplace that until a child goes to school he learns nothing that has not some direct bearing on his life. How he acquires this knowledge, is the question that will furnish the clew for natural school method. And the answer is, not by reading books or listening to explanations of the nature of fire or food, but by burning himself and feeding himself; that is, by doing things. Therefore, says the modern teacher, he ought to do things in school.

Education which ignores this vital impulse

furnished by the child is apt to be "academic," "abstract," in the bad sense of these words. If text-books are used as the sole material, the work is much harder for the teacher, for besides teaching everything herself she must constantly repress and cut off the impulses of the child towards action. Teaching becomes an external presentation lacking meaning and purpose as far as the child is concerned. Facts which are not led up to out of something which has previously occupied a significant place for its own sake in the child's life, are apt to be barren and dead. They are hieroglyphs which the pupil is required to study and learn while he is in school. It is only after the child has learned the same fact out of school, in the activities of real life, that it begins to mean anything to him. The number of isolated facts to which this can happen, which appear, say, in a geography textbook, are necessarily very small.

For the specialist in any one subject the material is all classified and arranged, but before it can be put in a child's text-book it must be simplified and greatly reduced in bulk. The thought provoking character is obscured and the organizing function disappears. The child's reasoning powers, the faculty of abstraction and generalization, are not adequately developed. This does not mean that the text-book must disappear, but that its function is changed. It becomes a guide for the pupil by which he may economize time and mistakes. The teacher and the book are no longer the only instructors; the hands, the eyes, the ears, in fact the whole body, become sources of information, while teacher and text-book become respectively the starter and the tester. No book or map is a substitute for personal experience; they cannot take the place of the actual journey. The mathematical formula for a falling body does not take the place of throwing stones or shaking apples from a tree.

Learning by doing does not, of course, mean the substitution of manual occupations or handwork for text-book studying. At the same time, allowing the pupils to do handwork whenever there is opportunity for it, is a great aid in holding the child's attention and interest.

Public School 45 of the Indianapolis school system is trying a number of experiments where the children may be said to be learning by doing. The work done is that required by the state curriculum, but the teachers are constantly finding new ways to prevent the work becoming a mere drill in text-book facts, or preparation for examinations. In the fifth grade, class activi-

Songs and games help arithmetic. (Public School 45, Indianapolis.)

ties were centered around a bungalow that the children were making. The boys in the class made the bungalow in their manual training hours. But before they started it every pupil had drawn a plan to scale of the house, and worked out, in their arithmetic period, the amount and cost of the lumber they would need, both for their own play bungalow and for a full sized one; they had done a large number of problems taken from the measurements for the house, such as finding the floor and wall areas and air space of each room, etc. The children very soon invented a family for their house and decided they would have them live on a farm. The arithmetic work was then based on the whole farm. First this was laid out for planting, plans were drawn to scale, and from information the children themselves gathered they made their own problems, basing them on their play farm: such as the size of the corn field, how many bushels of seeds would be needed to plant it; how big a crop they could expect, and how much profit. The children showed great interest and ingenuity in inventing problems containing the particular arithmetical process they were learning and which still would fit their farm. They built fences, cement sidewalks, a brick wall, did the marketing for the family, sold the butter, milk and eggs, and took out fire insurance. When they were papering the house the number of area problems connected with buying, cutting, and fitting the paper, were enough to give them all the necessary drill in measurement of areas.

English work centered in much the same way around the building of the bungalow and the life of its inhabitants. The spelling lessons came from the words they were using in connection with the building, etc. The plans for the completed bungalow, a description of the house and the furnishings, or the life of the family that dwelt in it, furnished inexhaustible material for compositions and writing lessons. Criticism of these compositions as they were read aloud to the class by their authors became work in rhetoric; even the grammar work became more interesting because the sentences were about the farm.

Art lessons were also drawn from the work the children were actually doing in building and furnishing the house. The pupils were very anxious that their house should be beautiful, so the color scheme for both the inside and outside furnished a number of problems in coloring and arrangement. Later they found large opportunities for design, in making wallpaper for the house, choosing and then decorating curtains and upholstery. Each pupil made his own design, and then the whole class decided which one they wanted to use. The pupils also designed and made clay tiles for the bathroom floor and wall, and planned and laid out a flower garden. The girls designed and made clothes for the doll inmates of the house. The whole class enjoyed their drawing lessons immensely because they drew each other posing as different members of the family in their different occupations on the farm. The work of this grade in expression consisted principally in dramatizations of the life on the farm which the children worked out for themselves. Not only were the children "learning by doing" in the sense that nearly all the school work centered around activities which had intrinsic meaning and value to the pupils, but most of the initiative for the work came from the children themselves. They made their own number problems; suggested the next step in the work on the house; criticised each other's compositions, and worked out their own dramatizations.

In almost all the grades in the school the pupils were conducting the recitations themselves whenever there was an opportunity. One pupil took charge of the class, calling on the others to recite; the teacher becoming a mere observer unless her interference was necessary to correct an error or keep the lesson to the point. When the class is not actually in charge of a pupil, every method is used to have the children do all the work, not to keep all the responsibility and initiative in the hands of the teacher. The pupils are encouraged to ask each other questions, to make their objections and corrections aloud, and to think out for themselves each problem as it comes up. This is not done by giving a class a set lesson in a textbook as an introduction to a new problem, but by suggesting the problem to the class and by means of questions and discussion, helped out whenever possible by actual experiments by the pupils, trying to bring out the solution of the problem, or at the least to give the pupil an understanding of what the problem is about before he sees it in print.

The method can be applied to all the classroom work, but one illustration taken from a geography lesson is especially suggestive. One grade was studying the Panama Canal, and had great difficulty in understanding the purpose or working of the canal, and especially the locks; in other words, they were not intellectually interested in what the teacher told them. She changed her method entirely and starting from the beginning, asked the class to pretend that Japan and the United States were at war, and that they were the Government at Washington and had to run the army. They at once became interested, and discovered that a canal across Panama was a necessity if the United States' ships were to arrive in the Pacific in time to defend the coast and the Hawaiian Islands. The mountain range seemed an impossible barrier, until the locks were explained to them again, when they seized the principle. Many of them, indeed, became so interested that they made models of locks at home to bring to school. They used the map freely and accurately in their interest in saving the country from invasion, but until one pupil asked why the United States did not actually build a canal across the Isthmus, they did not notice that their exciting game had anything to do with the puzzling facts that they had previously been trying to memorize from their text-book.

The teachers in the school make use of any illustrations from the practical life about them that fit in well with the work the grade is doing. Thus the third grade set up a parcel post system in their classroom, basing all their English and arithmetic work on it for some time, and learning to use a map and scales and weights as well. A retail shoe store gave the first grade plenty of work and fun, and games and dances with little songs have proved a great help in their number work. Most of the furniture in the school office was made by the big boys in their shop work, and several of the rooms are decorated with stencil designs the pupils made in their art lessons. The number work of the whole school is taught from the concrete side. The little children have boxes of tooth-picks and paper counters, which they use for adding and subtracting; the older pupils may tear paper or draw squares when they are learning a new process. The class is given something to do which illustrates the process to be taught; then the children themselves analyze what they have done and, as the last step, they do examples with pure numbers.

Many of the public schools of Chicago are also trying in every way possible to vitalize their work; to introduce into the curriculum material which the children themselves can handle and from which they may get their own lessons. This work is fitted into the regular curriculum; it is not dependent on any peculiarities of an individual teacher, but may be introduced throughout the entire system, just as text-books are now uniform through a large number of schools. The work has been applied principally in history and civics for the younger grades, but it is easy to imagine how the same sort of thing could be used in geography or some of the other subjects. The history in the younger grades is taught largely by means of sand tables. The children are perhaps studying the primitive methods of building houses, and on their sand table they build a brush house, a cave dwelling, a tree house, or an eskimo snow hut. The children themselves do all the work. The teacher steps in with advice and help only when necessary to prevent real errors, but the pupils are given the problem of the manufacture of the house they are studying, and are expected to solve it for themselves. Sand tables are used in the same way by a third grade in their study of the early history of Chicago. They mold the sand into a rough relief map of the neighborhood and then with twigs build the forts and log cabins of the first frontier settlement, with an Indian encampment just outside the stockade. They put real water in their lake and river, and float canoes in it. Other grades do the same thing with the history of transportation among the first settlers in this country, and with the logging and lumber industry.

The older grades are studying the government of their city, and make sand tables to illustrate the different departments of city government. One room has a life-saving station, with different types of boats, and life lines that work. Others have the telephone, mail carrier, and parcel posts systems, and a system of street cleaning of which the children are particularly proud, because they have copied conditions which they actually found in some of the alleys near the school buildings. Beside the alleys which were dirty, like those in the neighborhood, they have constructed a model alley with sanitary garbage appliances made on the best plane based on what the teacher has told them about systems in other cities.

In another building all the pupils above the fourth grade have organized into civic clubs. They divided the school district into smaller districts and one club took charge of each district, making surveys and maps of their own territory, counting lamp posts, alleys, and garbage cans, and the number of policemen, or going intensively into the one thing which interested them most. Then each club decided what they wanted to do for their own district and set out to accomplish it, whether it was the cleaning up of a bad alley or the better lighting of a street.

They used all the methods that an adult citizens' club would employ, writing letters to the city departments, calling at the City Hall, and besides actually went into the alleys and cleaned them up. The interest and enthusiasm of the pupils in this work was remarkable and they are now undertaking a campaign to get a playground for the school, by means of advertising and holding neighborhood meetings. The English work in these grades is based on the work of the clubs; the pupils keep track of the work they do, make maps and write letters.

Most of the hand and industrial work, which is not taught for strictly vocational purposes illustrates the principles which "learning by doing" stand for. Examples of this are to be found in nearly all schools to-day which aim to be progressive. Many school systems all over the country have tried having a printing press operated by pupils with great success. The presses were installed not to teach the pupils the different processes in the trade, but so that the children might themselves print some of the pamphlets, posters, or other papers that any school is constantly needing. Besides the interest that the pupils have shown in setting up the type, operating the presses, and getting out the printed matter, the work has proved itself especially valuable in the teaching of English. Type setting is an excellent method of drilling in spelling, punctuation, paragraphing, and grammar, for the fact that the copy is going to be printed furnishes a motive for eliminating mistakes which exercises written by a pupil for his teacher never provides. Proofreading is another exercise of the same sort. In such schools the press publishes practically all the printed matter that is needed during the year, including spelling lists, programs, and school papers.

Schools are trying all sorts of experiments to make the work in English concrete. The textbook method of teaching—learning rules and definitions and then doing exercises in their application—has proved unsuccessful. Every teacher is familiar with the story of the boy who wrote, "I have gone," on a piece of paper fifty times, in order to impress the correct form on his mind, and then on the bottom of the page left a note for the teacher beginning, "I have went home." A purpose in English work seems absolutely necessary, for the child sees no gain in efficiency in the things he is most interested in due to progress in isolated grammar or spelling. When the progress is brought about as a by-product of the scholars' other work the case is quite otherwise. Give him a reason for writing, for spelling, punctuating, and paragraphing, for using his verbs correctly, and improvement becomes a natural demand of experience. Mr. Wirt in the Gary, Ind., schools has found this so true that the regular English required by the state curriculum has been supplemented by "application periods in English." In these hours the class in carpentry or cooking discusses the English used in doing their work in those subjects, and corrects from the language point of view any written work done as part of their other activity. A pupil in one of these classes, who had been corrected for a mistake in grammar, was overheard saying, "Well, why didn't they tell us that in English?" to which her neighbor answered, "They did, but we didn't know what they were talking about."

In some schools as in the Francis Parker School, Chicago, and in the Cottage School at Riverside, Ill., English is not taught as a separate subject to the younger grades, but the pupils have compositions to write for their history lessons, keep records of their excursions, and of other work where they do not use text-books. The emphasis is put on helping the child to express his ideas; but such work affords ample opportunity for the drill in the required mechanics of writing. Grammar no longer appears as a separate subject in the Chicago public school curriculum; the teacher gives a lesson in grammar every time any one in the classroom talks and with every written exercise.

However, grammar can be given a purpose and made interesting even to eleven-year-old children, if the pupils are helped to make their own grammar and rules by doing their own analyzing as the first step instead of the last. This is being done with great success in the Phœbe Thorn Experimental School of Bryn Mawr College. Grammar had no place on the curriculum, but the pupils asked so many questions that their teacher decided to let them discover their own grammatical rules, starting from the questions they had asked. A few minutes were taken from the English hour two or three times a week for their lessons. At the end of three months the class could analyze any simple sentence, could tell a transitive from an intransitive verb instantly, and were thoroughly familiar with the rules governing the verb to be. The grammar lesson was one of the favorite lessons; the teacher and pupils together had invented a number of games to help their drill.

The pupils build the schoolhouses. (Interlaken School, Ind.)

For example, one child had a slip of paper pinned to her back describing a sentence in grammatical terms; the class made sentences that fitted the sentence, and the first pupil had to guess what her paper said. No text book was used in the work, and the teacher started with the sentence, called it a town, and by discussion helped the pupils to divide it up into districts—singular, plural, etc. Starting from this, they developed other grammatical rules. The general tendency in the progressive schools to-day, nevertheless, seems to be toward the elimination of the separate study of grammar, and toward making it and the remainder of the English work (with the exception of literature) a part of other subjects which the class is studying.

The motto of the boys' school at Interlaken, Ind., "To teach boys to live," is another way of saying, "learning by doing." Here this is accomplished, not so much by special devices to render the curriculum more vital and concrete, and by the abolition of text-books with the old-fashioned reservoir and pump relation of pupil and teacher, as by giving the boys an environment which is full of interesting things that need to be done.

The school buildings have been built by the

pupils, including four or five big log structures, the plans being drawn, the foundations dug and laid, and the carpentry and painting on the building done by boy labor. The electric light and heating plant is run by the boys, and all the wiring and bulbs were put in and are kept in repair by them. There is a six hundred acre farm, with a dairy, a piggery and hennery, and crops to be sowed and gathered. Nearly all this work is also done by pupils; the big boys driving the reapers and binders and the little boys going along to see how it is done. The inside of the houses are taken care of in the same way by the students. Each boy looks after his own room, and the work in the corridors and schoolrooms is attended to by changing shifts. There is a lake for swimming and canoeing, and plenty of time for the conventional athletics. Most of the boys are preparing for college, but this outdoor and manual work does not mean that they have to take any longer for their preparation than the boy in the city high school.

The school has also bought the local newspaper from the neighboring village and edits and prints a four-page weekly paper of local and school news. The boys gather the news, do much of the writing and all of the editing and printing, and are the business managers, getting advertisements and tending to the subscription list. The instructors in the English department give the boys any needed assistance. They do all these things, not because they want to know certain processes that will help them earn a living after they are through school, but because to use tools, to move from one kind of work to another, to meet different kinds of problems, to exercise outdoors, and to learn to supply one's daily needs are educating influences, which develop skill, initiative, independence, and bodily strength—in a word, character and knowledge.

Work in nature study is undergoing reorganization in many schools in all parts of the country. The attempt is to vitalize the work, so that pupils shall actually get a feeling for plants and animals, together with some real scientific knowledge, not simply the rather sentimental descriptions and rhapsodizings of literature. It is also different from the information gathering type of nature study, which is no more real science than is the literary type. Here the pupils are taught a large number of isolated facts, starting from material that the teacher gathers in a more or less miscellaneous way; they learn all about one object after another, each one unrelated to the others or to any general plan of work. Even though a child has gone over a large number of facts about the outdoor world, he gains little or nothing which makes nature itself more real or more understandable.

If nature study is turned into a science, the real material of the subject must be at hand for the students; there must be a laboratory, with provision for experimentation and observation. In the country this is easy, for nature is just outside the school doors and windows. The work can be organized in the complete way that has already been described in the schools at Fairhope and Columbia.

The Cottage School at Riverside, Ill., and the Little School in the Woods at Greenwich, Conn., both put a great deal of stress on their nature study work. At the former, the children have a garden where they plant early and late vegetables, so that they can use them for their cooking class in the spring and fall; the pupils do all the work here, plant, weed, and gather the things. Even more important is the work they do with animals. They have, for example, a rare bird that is as much a personality in the school life as any of the children, and the children, having cared for him and watched his growth and habits, have become much more interested in wild birds. In the backyard is a goat, the best liked thing on the place, which the children have raised from a little kid; and they still do all the work of caring for him. They are encouraged in every way to watch and report on the school pets and also on the animals they find in the woods.

In the Little School in the Woods at Greenwich outdoor work is the basis of the whole school organization. Nature study plays a large part in this. Groups of pupils take long walks through the woods in all seasons and weathers, learning the trees in all their dresses, and the flowers which come with each season. They learn to know the birds and their habits; they study insects in the same way, and learn about the stars. In fact, so much of their time is spent out of doors, that the pupils acquire first hand a large fund of knowledge of the world of nature in all its phases. The basis of this work, the director of the school calls Woodcraft; he believes that experience in the things the woodman does—riding, hunting, camping, scouting, mountaineering, Indian-craft, boating, etc.—will make strong, healthy, and independent young people with well developed characters and a true sense of the beauty of nature. The nature study then is a part of this other training. A teacher is always with the pupils, whether they are boating, walking, or gardening, to explain what they are doing and why, and to call their attention to the things about them. There is no doubt that the children in the school, even the very little ones, have a knowledge and appreciation of nature which are very rare even among country children.

Nature study in the big city, where the only plants are in parks and formal yards and where the only animals are the delivery horse and the alley cat, offers a very different problem. The teacher may well be puzzled as to the best way to teach her pupils to love nature when they never see it; or be doubtful as to the value of trying to develop powers of observation when the things which they are asked to observe not only do not play any part in the lives of the pupils but are in quite artificial surroundings. Yet while wild nature, the world of woods and fields and streams, is almost meaningless to the city bred child, there is plenty of material available to make nature a very real thing even for the child who has never seen a tree or cow. The modern teacher takes as a starting point anything that is familiar to the class; a caged canary, a bowl of gold fish, or the dusty trees on the playground, and starting from these she introduces the children to more and more of nature, until they can really get some idea of "the country" and the part it plays in the lives of every one. The vegetable garden is the obvious starting point for most city children; if they do not have tiny gardens in their own backyards, there is a neighbor who has, or they are interested to find out where the vegetables they eat come from and how they are grown.

Both in Indianapolis and Chicago, the public schools realize the value of this sort of work for the children. In Indianapolis, gardening is a regular department in the seventh and eighth grades and the high school. The city has bought a large tract of land far enough in town to be accessible, and any child who cannot have a garden at home may, by asking, have a garden plot together with lessons in the theory and practice of gardening. The plots are large enough for the pupils to gain considerable experience and to put into practice what they learn in the classroom. Both boys and girls have the gardens, and are given credit for work in them just as for other work. All through the school system every attempt is made to arouse an interest in gardening. From the first grade on, statistics are kept of the numbers of children with gardens at home, whether they are vegetable or flower gardens, and what is grown. Seeds are given to the children who wish to grow new things, and the child is supposed to account to his grade for the use he has made of his garden.

This work has become a matter of course in many rural districts; every one is familiar with the "corn clubs" among the school children of the South and West, and the splendid example they have set the farmers as to the possibilities of the soil. In many small towns seeds are given to the children who want gardens, and in the fall a competitive flower and vegetable show is held, where prizes are given, as a means of keeping track of the work and arousing community interest. It is true that most of these efforts have been grafted on to the schools by the local agricultural interests, in an effort to improve the crops and so increase the wealth of the neighborhood; but local school boards are beginning to take the work over, and it is no less real nature study work because of its utilitarian color. It may be made a means of making a real science of nature study; in no way does it hinder the teaching of the beauty and usefulness of nature, which was the object of the old-fashioned study. In fact, it is the strongest weapon the school can make use of for this purpose. Every one, and children especially, enjoy and respect most the things about which their fund of knowledge is largest. The true value of anything is most apparent to the person who knows something about it. Familiarity with growing things and with the science of getting food supplies for a people, cannot fail to be a big influence towards habits of industry and observation, for only the gardener who watches all the stages and conditions of his garden, seeking constantly for causes, will be successful. Added to this is the purely economic value of having our young people grow up with a real respect for the farmer and his work, a respect which should counteract that overwhelming flow of population toward congested cities.

The work in the Chicago public schools has not been organized as it is in Indianapolis, but in some districts of the city a great deal of emphasis is put on nature study work through gardens. Many of the schools have school gardens where all the children get an opportunity to do real gardening, these gardens being used as the basis for the nature study work, and the children getting instruction in scientific gardening besides. The work is given a civic turn; that is to say, the value of the gardens to the child and to the neighborhood is demonstrated: to the child as a means of making money or helping his family by supplying them with vegetables, to the community in showing how gardens are a means of cleaning up and beautifying the neighborhood. If the residents want their backyards and empty lots for gardens, they are not going to throw rubbish into them or let other people do so. Especially in the streets around one school has this work made a difference. Starting with the interest and effort of the children, the whole community has become tremendously interested in starting gardens, using every bit of available ground. The district is a poor one and, besides transforming the yards, the gardens have been a real economic help to the people. With the help of one school a group of adults in the district hired quite a large tract of land outside the city and started truck gardens. The experiment was a great success. Inexperienced city dwellers, by taking advantage of the opportunities for instruction which the school could offer, were able to plan and do the work and make the garden a success from the start. The advantage to the school was just as great, for a large group of foreign parents came into close touch with it, discovered that it was a real force in the neighborhood, and that

Real gardens for city nature study. (Public School 45, Indianapolis.)

they could coöperate with it. This element of the population usually stands quite aloof from the school its children go to, through timidity and ignorance, or simply through feeling that it is an institution above them.

The impetus to "civic nature study" in Chicago, aside from the district just described, has come largely from the Chicago Teachers' College, where the teacher of biology has devoted himself especially to working out this problem. In addition to the familiar gardening work, with especial attention to the organization of truck gardening, plants are grown in the classroom for purposes of developing appreciation of beauty, scientific illustration, and assistance in geography. But plants are selected with special reference to local conditions, and with the desire to furnish a stimulus to beautifying the pupils' own environment. For it is found that the scientific principles of botany can be taught by means of growing plants which are adapted to home use as well as by specimens selected on abstract scientific grounds. By making a special study of the parks, playgrounds, and yards of their surroundings, the children learn what can be done to beautify their city, and secure an added practical motive for acquiring information. They keep pets in the schoolroom, such as white mice, fish, birds, and rabbits. While these are utilized, of course, for illustrating principles of animal structure and physiology, they are also employed to teach humaneness to animals and a general sympathy for animal life. This is easy, for children are naturally even more interested in animals than in plants, and the animals become real individualities to the children whose needs are to be respected. As the effect of conditions upon the health and vigor of their pets is noted, there is a natural growth of interest in questions of personal hygiene.

It will be observed that while nature study is used to instill the elements of science, its chief uses are to cultivate a sympathetic understanding of the place of plants and animals in life and to develop emotional and æsthetic interest. In the larger cities the situation is very different from that of rural life and the country village. There are thousands of children who believe that cement and bricks are the natural covering of the ground, trees and grass being to them the unusual and artificial thing. Their thoughts do not go beyond the fact that milk and butter and eggs come from the store; cows and chickens are unknown to them—so much so that in a recent reunion of old settlers in a congested district of New York one of the greatest curiosities was a live cow imported from the country. Under such circumstances, it is difficult to make the scientific problems of nature study of vital interest. There are no situations of the children's experience into which the facts and principles enter as a matter of course. Even the weather is tempered and the course of the changing seasons has no special effect upon the lives of the pupils, save upon the need for greater warmth in winter. Nature study in the city is like one of the fine arts, such as painting or music; its value is æsthetic rather than directly practical. Nature is such a small factor in the activities of the children that it is hard to give it much "disciplinary" value, save as it is turned to civic ends. A vague feeling for this state of affairs probably accounts for much of the haphazard and half-hearted nature study teaching which goes on in city schools. There is a serious problem in finding material for city children which will do for observation what the facts of nature accomplish in the case of rural children.

A valuable experiment with this end in view is carried on in the little "Play School" taught by Miss Pratt in one of the most congested districts of New York City. Nature study is not taught at all to these little children. If they go to the park or have pets and plant flowers it is because these things make good play material, because they are beautiful and interesting; if the children ask questions and want to know more about them, so much the better. Instead of telling them about leaves and grass, cows and butterflies, and hunting out the rare opportunities for the children to observe them, use is made of the multitudes of things which the children see about them in the streets and in their homes. The new building going up across the street furnishes just as much for observation and questioning as does the park, and is a much more familiar sight to the children. They find out how the men get the bricks and mortar to the upper floors; they see the sand cart unloading; possibly one child knows that the driver has been to the river to get the sand from a boat. They notice the delivery man going through the streets, and find out where he got the bread to take to their mothers. They see the children on the playground and learn that besides the fun they have, the playing is good for their bodies. They walk to the river and see the ferries carrying people back and forth and the coal barges unloading. All these facts are more closely related to them than the things of country life; hence it is more important that they understand their meaning and their relation to their own lives, while acuteness of observation is just as well trained. Such work is also equally valuable as a foundation for the science and geography the pupils will study later on. Besides awakening their curiosity and faculties of observation, it shows them the elements of the social world, which the later studies are meant to explain.

The Elementary School at Columbia, Missouri, has arranged its curriculum according to the same principle. All the material from nature which the children use and study they find near the school or their homes, and their study of the seasons and the weather is made from day to day, as the Columbia weather and seasons change. Even more important is the work the children do in studying their own town, their food, clothing, and houses, so that the basis of the study is not instruction given by the teacher but what the children themselves have been able to find out on excursions and by keeping their eyes open. The material bears a relation to their own lives, and so is the more available for teaching children how to live. The reasons for teaching such things to the city bred child are the same as those for teaching the country child the elements of gardening and the possibilities of the local soil. By understanding his own environment child or adult learns the measure of the beauty and order about him, and respect for real achievement, while he is laying the foundations for his own control of the environment.

CHAPTER V

PLAY

ALL peoples at all times have depended upon plays and games for a large part of the education of children, especially of young children. Play is so spontaneous and inevitable that few educational writers have accorded to it in theory the place it held in practice, or have tried to find out whether the natural play activities of children afforded suggestions that could be adopted within school walls. Plato among the ancients and Froebel among the moderns are the two great exceptions. From both Rousseau and Pestalozzi, Froebel learned the principle of education as a natural development. Unlike both of these men, however, he loved intellectual system and had a penchant for a somewhat mystical metaphysics. Accordingly we find in both his theory and practice something of the same inconsistency noted in Pestalozzi.

It is easier to say natural development than to find ways for assuring it. There is much that is "natural" in children which is also naturally obnoxious to adults. There are many manifestations which do not seem to have any part in helping on growth. Impatient desire for a method which would cover the whole ground, and be final so as to be capable of use by any teacher, led Froebel, as it has led so many others, into working out alleged "laws" of development which were to be followed irrespective of the varying circumstances and experiences of different children. The orthodox kindergarten, which has often been more Froebellian than Froebel himself, followed these laws; but now we find attempts to return to the spirit of his teaching, with more or less radical changes in its letter.

While Froebel's own sympathy with children and his personal experience led him to emphasize the instinctive expressions of child-life, his philosophy led him to believe that natural development consisted in the *un*folding of an absolute and universal principle already *en*folded in the child. He believed also that there is an exact correspondence between the general properties of external objects and the unfolding qualities of mind, since both were manifestations of the same absolute reality. Two practical consequences followed which often got the upper hand of his interest in children on their own account. One was that, since the law of development could be laid down in general, it is not after all so important to study children in the concrete to find out what natural development consists in. If they vary from the requirements of the universal law so much the worse for them, not for the "law." Teachers were supposed to have the complete formula of development already in their hands. The other consequence was that the presentation and handling, according to prescribed formulæ, of external material, became the method in detail of securing proper development. Since the general relations of these objects, especially the mathematical ones, were manifestations of the universal principle behind development, they formed the best means of bringing out the hidden existence of the same principle in the child. Even the spontaneous plays of children were thought to be educative not because of what they are, directly in themselves, but because they symbolize some law of universal being. Children should gather, for example, in a circle, not because a circular grouping is convenient for social and practical purposes, but because the circle is a symbol of infinity which will tend to evoke the infinite latent in the child's soul.

The efforts to return to Froebel's spirit referred to above have tried to keep the best in his contributions. His emphasis upon play, dramatization, songs and story telling, which involve the constructive use of material, his deep sense of the importance of social relations among the children—these things are permanent contributions which they retain. But they are trying with the help of the advances of psychological knowledge since Froebel's time and of the changes in social occupations which have taken place to utilize these factors directly, rather than indirectly, through translation into a metaphysics, which, even if true, is highly abstract. In another respect they are returning to Froebel himself, against an alteration in his ideas introduced by many of his disciples. These followers have set up a sharp contrast between play and useful activity or work, and this has rendered the practices of their kindergartens more symbolic and sentimental than they otherwise would have been. Froebel himself emphasized the desirability of children sharing in social occupations quite as much as did Pestalozzi—whose school he had visited. He says, for example, "The young, growing human being should be trained early for outer work, for creative and productive activities. Lessons through and by work, through and from life, are the most impressive and the most intelligible, the most continuous and progressive, in themselves and in their effect upon the learner. Every child, boy and youth, whatever his position and condition in life, should devote, say, at least one or two hours a day to some serious active occupation constructing some definite external piece of work. It would be a most wholesome arrangement in school to establish actual working hours similar to existing study hours, and it will surely come to this." In the last sentence, Froebel showed himself a true prophet of what has been accomplished in some of the schools such as we are dealing with in this book.

Schools all over the country are at present making use of the child's instinct for play, by using organized games, toy making, or other construction based on play motives as part of the regular curriculum. This is in line with the vitalization of the curriculum that is going on in the higher grades by making use of the environment of the child outside the schoolroom. If the most telling lessons can be given children through bringing into the school their occupations in their free hours, it is only natural to use play as a large share of the work for the youngest pupils. Certainly the greatest part of the lives of very young children is spent in playing, either games which they learn from older children or those of their own invention. The latter usually take the form of imitations of the occupations of their elders. All little children think of playing house, doctor, or soldier, even if they are not given toys which suggest these games; indeed, half of the joy of playing comes from finding and making the necessary things. The educational value of this play is obvious. It teaches the children about the world they live in. The more they play the more elaborate becomes their paraphernalia, the whole game being a fairly accurate picture of the daily life of their parents in its setting, clothed in the language and bearing of the children. Through their games they learn about the work and play of the grown-up world. Besides noticing the elements which make up this world, they find out a good deal about the actions and processes that are necessary to keep it going.

While this is of real value in teaching the child how to live, it is evident as well that it supplies a strong influence against change. Imitative plays tend, by the training of habit and the turn they give to the child's attention and thoughts, to make his life a replica of the

(1) Making a town, instead of doing gymnastic exercises.
(Teachers College Playground, N. Y. City.)

(2) Gymnasium dances in sewing-class costumes.
(Howland School, Chicago.)

life of his parents. In playing house children are just as apt to copy the coarseness, blunders, and prejudices of their elders as the things which are best. In playing, they notice more carefully and thus fix in their memory and habits, more than if they simply lived it indifferently, the whole color of the life around them. Therefore, while imitative games are of great educational value in the way of teaching the child to notice his environment and some of the processes that are necessary for keeping it going, if the environment is not good the child learns bad habits and wrong ways of thinking and judging, ways which are all the harder to break because he has fixed them by living them out in his play.

Modern kindergartens are beginning to realize this more and more. They are using play, the sort of games they find the children playing outside of school hours, not only as a method of making work interesting to the children, but for the educational value of the activities it involves, and for giving the children the right sort of ideals and ideas about every day life. Children who play house and similar games in school, and have toys to play with and the material to make the things they need in their play, will play house at home the way they played it in school. They will forget to imitate the loud and coarse things they see at home, their attention will be centered on problems which were designed by the school to teach better aims and methods.

The kindergarten of the Teachers' College of Columbia University could hardly be recognized as a kindergarten at all by a visitor who was thinking of the mechanism of instruction worked out by Froebel's disciples. The kindergarten is part of the training school of the university, and from the start has been considered as a real part of the school system, as the first step in an education, not as a more or less unnecessary "extra." With a view to laying a permanent basis for higher education, the authorities have been developing a curriculum that should make use of whatever was of real worth in existing systems of education and in the experiments tried by themselves. To find what is of real worth, experiments have been conducted, designed to answer the following questions: "Among the apparently aimless and valueless spontaneous activities of the child is it possible to discover some which may be used as the point of departure for ends of recognized worth? Are there some of these crude expressions which, if properly directed, may develop into beginnings of the fine and industrial arts? How far does the preservation of the individuality and freedom of the child demand self-initiated activities? Is it possible for the teacher to set problems or ends sufficiently childlike to fit in with the mode of growth, and to inspire their adoption with the same fine enthusiasm which accompanies the self-initiated ones?''

The result showed that the best success came when the children's instinctive activities were linked up with social interests and experiences. The latter center, with young children, in their home. Their personal relations are of the greatest importance to them. Children's intense interest in dolls is a sign of the significance attached to human relations. The doll thus furnished a convenient starting point. With this as a motive, the children have countless things they wish to do and make. Hand and construction work thus acquired a real purpose, with the added advantage of requiring the child to solve a problem. The doll needs clothes; the whole class is eager to make them, but the children do not know how to sew or even cut cloth. So they start with paper and scissors, and make patterns, altering and experimenting on the doll for themselves, receiving only suggestions or criticisms from the teacher. When they have made successful patterns, they choose and cut the cloth, and then learn to sew it. If the garments are not wholly successful, the class has had a great deal of fun making them, and has had the training that comes from working towards a definite end, besides acquiring as much control over scissors, paper, and needle, and manual dexterity as would accrue from the conventional paper cutting, pricking, and sewing exercises.

The doll needs a house. In a corner of the room there is a great chest of big blocks, so large that it takes the whole class to build the house, and then it is not done in one day. There are flat long blocks like boards for the walls and roof, and square blocks for the foundations and window frames. When the house is done, it is big enough for two or three children to go into to play with the doll. One readily sees that it has taken a great deal of hard thinking and experimenting to make a house that would really stand up and serve such uses. Then the house needs furniture; the children learn to handle tools in fashioning tables, chairs, and beds, from blocks of wood and thin boards. Getting the legs on a table is an especially interesting problem to the class, and over and over again they have discovered for themselves how it can be done. Dishes for the doll family furnish the motive for clay modeling and decoration. Dressing and undressing the dolls is an occupation the children never tire of, and it furnishes excellent practice in buttoning and unbuttoning and tying bows.

The changing seasons of the year and the procession of outdoor games they bring furnish other motives for production that meet a real need of the children. In the spring-time they want marbles and tops, in the fall, kites; the demand for wagons is not limited to any one season. Whenever possible the children are allowed to solve their own problems. If they want marbles they experiment until they find a good way to make them round, while if they are making something more difficult where the whole process is obviously beyond them, they are helped. This help, however, never takes the form of dictation as to how to perform each step in its order, for the object of the work is to train the child's initiative and self-reliance, to teach him to think straight by having him work on his own problems. The little carts which the older children make would be beyond them if they had to plan and shape the material for themselves; but when they are given the sawed boards and round pieces for wheels, they find out by trying how they can be put together, and thus make usable little wagons. Making bags for their marbles, and aprons to protect their clothes while they are painting the dolls' furniture or washing the dishes after lunch, offer additional opportunities for sewing.

From the needs of an individual doll the child's interest naturally develops to the needs of a family and then of a whole community. With paper dolls and boxes, the children make and furnish dolls' houses for themselves, until all together they produce an entire village. On their sand table the whole class may make a town with houses and streets, fences and rivers, trees and animals for the gardens. In fact, the play of the children furnishes more opportunity for making things than there is time for in the school year. This construction work not only fills the children with the interest and enthusiasm they always show for any good game, but teaches them the use of work. In supplying the needs of the dolls and their own games, they are supplying in miniature the needs of society, and are acquiring control over the tools that society actually uses in meeting these wants. Boys and girls alike take the same interest in all these occupations, whether they are sewing and playing with dolls, or marble making and carpentry. The idea that certain games and occupations are for boys and others for girls is a purely artificial one that has developed as a reflection of the conditions existing in adult life. It does not occur to a boy that dolls are not just as fascinating and legitimate a plaything for him as for his sister, until some one puts the idea into his head.

The program of this kindergarten is not devoted exclusively to play construction. It occupies the place of the paper folding, pricking and sewing and the object lesson work of the older kindergartens, leaving plenty of time every day to try their playthings and to take care of their little gardens out of doors, as well as for group games, stories and songs.

An interesting application of the play motive is being tried at the Teachers' College play ground, by the same teachers who are conducting the kindergarten. There is an outdoor playground for the use of the younger grades after school hours. Instead of spending their time doing gymnastic exercises or playing group games the children are making a town. They use large packing cases for houses and stores, two or three children taking care of each one; and have worked out quite an elaborate town organization, with a telephone, mail and police service, a bank to coin money, and ingenious schemes for keeping the cash in circulation. Much of the time is spent in carpentry work, building and repairing the houses and making wagons, furniture for the houses, or stock for the two stores. The work affords almost as much physical exercise as the ordinary sort of playground. It keeps the children busy and happy in a much more effective way, for besides healthy play in the open air they are learning to take a useful and responsible share in a community.

A kindergarten conducted along the same lines exists in Pittsburgh as part of the city university. It is called "The School of Childhood," and emphasizes the healthy physical development of the children. The work is centered around the natural interests of children; and while they apparently do not do as much construction work as in the Teachers' College kindergarten, there is more individual play. The writer has not visited the school, but it seems to embrace a number of novel elements that ought to be suggestive to any one interested in educational experiments.

The "Play School" conducted by Miss Pratt in New York City organizes all the work around the play activities of little children. Quoting

Miss Pratt, her plan is: "To offer an opportunity to the child to pick up the thread of life in his own community, and to express what he gets in an individual way. The experiment concerns itself with getting subject-matter first hand, and it is assumed that the child has much information to begin with, that he is adding to it day by day, that it is possible to direct his attention so that he may get his information in a more related way; and with applying such information to individual schemes of play with related toys and blocks as well as expressing himself through such general means as drawing, dramatization, and spoken language."

The children are of kindergarten age and come from homes where the opportunities for real activity are limited. Each child has floor space of his own with a rug, and screens to isolate him sufficiently so that his work is really individual. There is a small work shop in the room where the pupils can make or alter things they need in their play. The tools are full size, and miscellaneous scraps of wood are used. In cupboards and shelves around the room are all sorts of material: toys, big and little blocks, clay, pieces of cloth, needle and thread, and a set of Montessori material. Each child has scissors, paper, paints, and pencil of his own, and is free to use all the material as he chooses. He selects either isolated objects he wants to make, or lays out some larger construction, such as a railroad track and stations, or a doll's house, or a small town or farm, and then from the material at hand works out his own execution of his idea. One piece of work often lasts over several days, and involves considerable incidental construction, such as tracks and signals, clay dishes, furniture or new clothes for the doll. The rôle of the teacher is to teach the pupil processes and control of tools, not in a prearranged scale but as they are needed in construction. The teacher has every opportunity to see the individual's weaknesses and abilities and so to check or stimulate at the proper time. Besides the motor control which the pupils develop through their handling of material, they are constantly increasing their ingenuity and initiative.

The elements of number work are taught in connection with the construction; and if a child shows a desire to make letters or signs in connection with his other work, he is helped and shown how. The toys used are particularly good. There are flat wooden dolls about half an inch thick, men, women, and children, whose joints bend so that they will stay

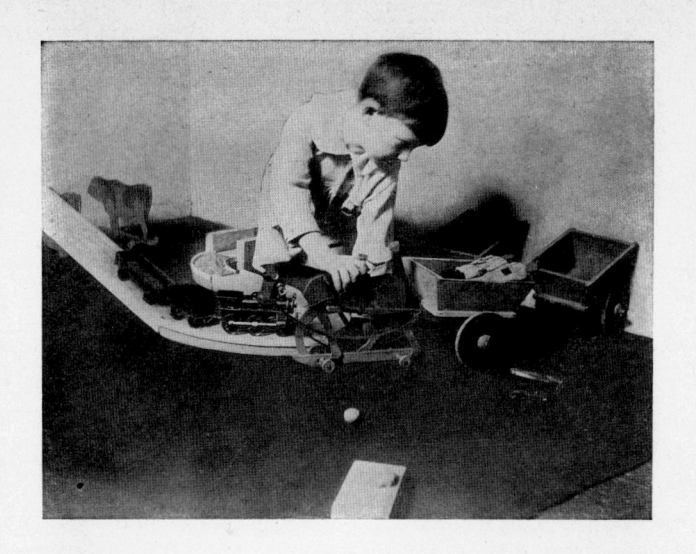

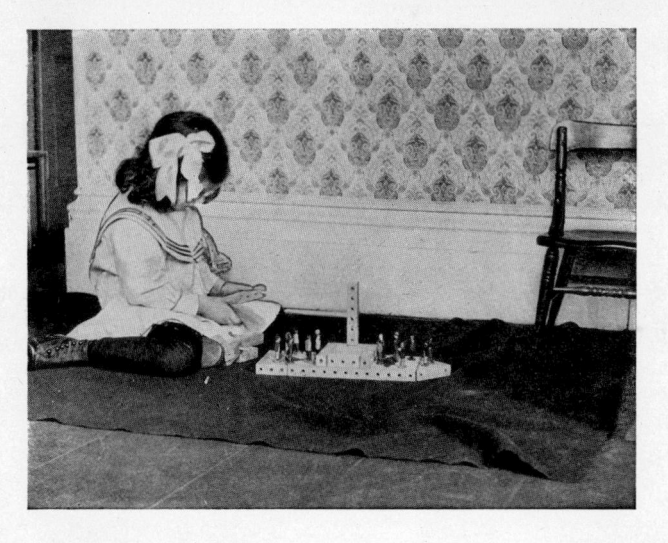

Constructing in miniature the things they see around them.
(Play School, New York City.)

in any position; all sorts of farm animals and two or three kinds of little wagons that fit the dolls; quantities of big blocks that fasten together with wooden pegs, so that the houses and bridges do not fall down. Everything is strongly made on the simplest plan, so that material can be used not only freely but also effectively. Each success is a stimulus to new and more complicated effort. There is no discouragement from slipshod stuff. The pupils take care of the toys themselves, getting them out and putting them away. They also care for the classroom and serve their midmorning luncheon. This work, coupled with the fact that the constructions are almost always miniature copies of the things that the pupils see in their community, saves the work from any hint of artificiality. The children's constructions grow out of the observations already spoken of (p. 100), and give a motive for talking over what they have seen and making new, more extensive and more accurate observations.

The natural desire of children to play can, of course, be made the most of in the lowest grades, but there is one element of the play instinct which schools are utilizing in the higher grades—that is, the instinct for dramatization, for make-believe in action. All children love to pretend that they are some body or thing other than themselves; they love to make a situation real by going through the motions it suggests. Abstract ideas are hard to understand; the child is never quite sure whether he really understands or not. Allow him to act out the idea and it becomes real to him, or the lack of understanding is shown in what is done. Action is the test of comprehension. This is simply another way of saying that learning by doing is a better way to learn than by listening—the difference of dramatization from the work already described lies in the things the child is learning. He is no longer dealing with material where *things* are needed to carry an act to a successful result, but with *ideas* which need action to make them real. Schools are making use of dramatization in all sorts of different ways to make teaching more concrete. For older children dramatization is used principally in the strict sense of the word; that is, by having pupils act in plays, either as a means of making the English or history more real, or simply for the emotional and imaginative value of the work. With the little children it is used as an aid in the teaching of history, English, reading, or arithmetic, and is often combined with other forms of activity.

PLAY

Many schools use dramatization as a help in teaching the first steps of any subject, especially in the lower grades. A first year class, for example, act the subject-matter of their regular reading lesson, each child having the part of one of the characters of the story, animal or person. This insures an idea of the situation as a whole, so that reading ceases to be simply an attempt to recognize and pronounce isolated words and phrases. Moreover, the interest of the situation carries children along, and enlists attention to difficulties of phraseology which might, if attacked as separate things, be discouraging. The dramatic factor is a great assistance in the expressive side of reading. Teachers are always having to urge children to read "naturally," "to read as they talk." But when a child has no motive for communication of what he sees in the text, knowing as he does that the teacher has the book and can tell it better than he can, even the naturalness tends to be forced and artificial. Every observer knows how often children who depart from humdrum droning, learn to exhibit only a superficial breathless sort of liveliness and a make-believe animation. Dramatization secures both attention to the thought of the text and a spontaneous endeavor, free from pretense and self-consciousness, to speak loudly enough to be heard and to enunciate distinctly. In the same way, children tell stories much more effectively when they are led to visualize for themselves the actions going on, than when they are simply repeating something as a part of the school routine. When children are drawing scenes involving action and posture, it is found that prior action is a great assistance. In the case of a pose of the body, the child who has done the posing is often found to draw better than those who have merely looked on. He has got the "feel" of the situation, which readily influences his hand and eye in the subsequent reproduction. In the early grades when pupils fail in a concrete problem in arithmetic, it is frequently found that resort to "acting out" the situation supplies all the assistance needed. The real difficulty was not with the numbers but in failure to grasp the meaning of the situation in which the numbers were to be used.

In the upper grades, literature and history, as already indicated, are often reënforced by dramatic activities. A sixth grade in Indianapolis engaged in dramatizing "Sleeping Beauty," not merely composed the words and the stage directions, but also wrote songs and the music for them. Such concentration on a single purpose of studies usually pursued independently stimulates work in each. Literary expression is less monotonous, the phrasing of an idea more delicate and flexible, than when composition is an end in itself; and while of course the music is not likely to be remarkable, it almost always has a freshness and charm exceeding that which could be attained from the same pupils if they were merely writing music.

A shoe store in the second grade furnished the basis of the work for several days. The children set up a shop and chose pupils to take the part of the shoe clerk, the shoemaker, and the family going to buy shoes. Then they acted out the story of a mother and children going to the store for shoes. Arithmetic and English lessons were based on the store, and the class wrote stories about it. This same class sang and acted out to a simple tune a little verse about the combinations that make ten. The same pupils were doing problems in mental arithmetic that were much beyond the work usually found in a second grade, adding almost instantly numbers like 74 and 57. They probably could not have gone so rapidly if they had not had so much of the dramatization work. It served to make their abstract problems seem real. In doing problems about Mrs. Baldwin's shoes they had come to think of numbers as having some meaning and purpose, so that when a problem in pure numbers was given they did not approach it with misgivings and uncertainty. One of the fifth grades had installed a parcel post office; they made money and stamps and brought bundles to school, then they played post office; two boys took the part of postmen, weighed the packages, looked up the rate of postage, and gave change for the customers. Tables of weights ceased to be verbal forms to be memorized; consultation of the map was a necessity; the multiplication table was a necessity; the system and order required in successful activity were impressed.

The Francis Parker School is one of many using the dramatic interest of the pupils as an aid in teaching history. The fourth grade studies Greek history, and the work includes the making of a Greek house, and writing poems about some Greek myth. The children make Greek costumes and wear them every day in the classroom. To quote Miss Hall, who teaches this grade: "They play sculptor and make clay statuettes of their favorite gods and mould figures to illustrate a story. They model Mycenæ in sand-pans, ruin it, cover it, and become the excavators who bring its treasures to light again. They write prayers to Dionysius and stories such as they think Orpheus might have sung. They play Greek games and wear Greek costumes, and are continually acting out stories or incidents which please them. To-day as heroes of Troy, they have a battle at recess time with wooden swords and barrel covers. In class time, with prayers and dances and extempore song, they hold a Dionysiac festival. Again, half of them are Athenians and half of them Spartans in a war of words as to which city is more to be desired. Or they are freemen of Athens, replying spiritedly to the haughty Persian message." Besides these daily dramatizations, they write and act for the whole school a little play which illustrates some incident of history that has particularly appealed to them. History taught in this way to little children acquires meaning and an emotional content; they appreciate the Greek spirit and the things which made a great people. The work so becomes a part of their lives that it is remembered as any personal experience is retained, not as texts are committed to memory to be recited upon.

The Francis Parker School takes advantage of the social value of dramatizations in its morning exercises. Studying alone out of a book is an isolated and unsocial performance; the pupil may be learning the words before him, but he is not learning to act with other people, to control and arrange his actions and thought so that other persons have an equal opportunity to express themselves in a shared experience. When the classes represent by action what they have learned from books, all the members have a part, so that they learn to cherish socially, as well as to develop, powers of expression and of dramatic and emotional imagery. When they act in front of the whole school they get the value of the work for themselves individually and help the growth of a spirit of unity and coöperation in the entire school. All the children, big and little, become interested in the sort of thing that is going on in the other grades, and learn to appreciate effort that is simple and sincere, whether it comes from the first grade or the seniors in high school. In their efforts to interest the whole school the actors learn to be simple and direct, and acquire a new respect for their work by seeing its value for others. Summaries of the work in different subjects are given in the morning exercises by any grade which thinks it has something to say that would interest the other children. The dramatic element is sometimes small, as in the descriptions of excursions, of curious processes in arithmetic or of some topic in geography; but the children always have to think clearly and speak well, or their audience will not understand them, and maps or diagrams and all sorts of illustrative material are introduced as much as possible. Other exercises, such as the Greek play written by the fourth grade, or a dramatization of one of Cicero's orations against Cataline, are purely dramatic in their interest.

The production of plays by graduating classes or for some specific purpose is of course a well-known method of interesting pupils or advertising a school. But recently schools have been giving plays and festivals for their educational value as well as for their interest to children and the public. The valuable training which comes from speaking to an audience, using the body effectively and working with other pupils for a common end, is present, whatever the nature of the play; and schools usually try to have their productions of some literary value. But until recently the resources of the daily work of the pupils for dramatic purposes have been overlooked. Being for purposes of public entertainment, plays were added on after school hours. But schools are beginning to utilize this natural desire of young people to "act something" for amplifying the curriculum. In many schools where dramatization of a rather elaborate character is employed for public performances, the subject-matter is now taken from English and history, while writing the play supplies another English lesson. The rehearsals take the place of lessons in expression and elocution, and involve self-control. The stage settings and costumes are made in the shop and art periods, the planning and management being done by the pupils, the teacher helping enough to prevent blunders and discouragement. At Riverside one of the classes had been reading Tolstoi's "Where Love Is There Is God" for their work in literature. They rewrote the story as a play and rehearsed it in their English lessons, the whole class acting as coach and critic. As their interest grew they made costumes and arranged a stage setting and finally gave the play to an audience of the school and its friends. At another time the English class gave an outdoor performance of a sketch which they had written, based on the Odyssey. The American history class at the Speyer School give a play which they write about some incident in pioneer history. During the rehearsal nearly all the children try the parts, quite regardless of sex or other qualifications, and the whole class chooses the final cast. The fifth grade was studying

Using the child's dramatic instinct to teach history. (Cottage School, Riverside, Ill.)

Irving's "Sketch Book" in connection with its history and literature work, and dramatized the story of Rip Van Winkle, doing all its own coaching and costuming.

The Howland School, one of the public schools of Chicago situated in a foreign district, gave a large festival play during the past year. The principal wrote and arranged a pageant illustrating the story of Columbus, and the whole school took part in the acting. The story gave a simple outline of the life of Columbus. A few tableaux were added about some of the most striking events in pioneer history, arranged to bring out the fact that this country is a democracy. The children made their own costumes for the most part, and all the dances they had learned during the year in gymnasium were introduced. Thus the whole exhibition presented a very good picture of the outline of our history and the spirit of the country, and at the same time offered an interesting summary of the year's work. Its value as a unifying influence in a foreign community was considerable, for besides teaching the children something of the history of their new country, it gave the parents, who made up the audience, an opportunity to see what the school could do for their children and the neighborhood. The patriotic value of such exercises is greater than the daily flag salute or patriotic poem, for the children understand what they are supposed to be enthusiastic about, as they see before them the things which naturally arouse patriotic emotions.

Exercises to commemorate holidays or seasons are more interesting and valuable than the old-fashioned entertainment where individual pupils recited poems, and adults made speeches, for they concentrate in a social expression the work of the school. The community is more interested because parents know that their own children have had their share in the making of the production, and the children are more interested because they are working in groups on something which appeals to them and for which they are responsible. The graduating exercises at many schools are now of a kind to present in a dramatic review the regular work of the year. Each grade may take part, presenting a play which they have written for work in English, dancing some of the folk or fancy dances they have learned in gymnasium, etc. Many schools have a Thanksgiving exercise in which different grades give scenes from the first Thanksgiving at Plymouth, or present dramatic pictures of the harvest festivals of different nations. In similar fashion Christmas entertainments are often made up of songs, poems and readings by children from different grades, or by the whole grade, which have been arranged in the English and music classes. The possibilities for plays, festivals, and pageants arranged on this plan are endless; for it is always possible to find subject-matter which will give the children just as much training in reading, spelling, history, literature, or even some phases of geography, as would dry Gradgrind facts of a routine text-book type.

CHAPTER VI

FREEDOM AND INDIVIDUALITY

The reader has undoubtedly been struck by the fact that in all of the work described, pupils must have been allowed a greater amount of freedom than is usually thought compatible with the necessary discipline of a schoolroom. To the great majority of teachers and parents the very word school is synonymous with "discipline," with quiet, with rows of children sitting still at desks and listening to the teacher, speaking only when they are spoken to. Therefore a school where these fundamental characteristics are lacking must of necessity be a poor school; one where pupils do not learn anything, where they do just as they please, quite regardless of what they please, even though it be harmful to the child himself or disagreeable to his classmates and the teacher.

There is a certain accumulation of facts that every child must acquire or else grow up to be illiterate. These facts relate principally to adult life; therefore it is not surprising that the

FREEDOM AND INDIVIDUALITY 133

pupil is not interested in them, while it is the duty of the school to see that he knows them nevertheless. How is this to be done? Obviously by seating the children in rows, far enough apart so that they cannot easily talk to each other, and hiring the most efficient person available to teach the facts; to tell them to the child, and have him repeat them often enough so that he can reasonably be expected to remember them, at least until after he is "promoted."

Again, children should be taught to obey; efficiency in doing as one is told is a useful accomplishment, just as the doing of distasteful and uninteresting tasks is a character builder. The pupil should be taught to "respect" his teacher and learning in general; and how can he be taught this lesson if he does not sit quietly and receptively in the face of both? But if he will not be receptive, he must at least be quiet, so that the teacher can teach him anyway. The very fact that the pupil so often is lawless, destructive, rude and noisy as soon as restraint is removed proves, according to the advocates of "discipline" by authority, that this is the only way of dealing with the child, since without such restraint the child would behave all day long as he does when it is removed for a few uncertain minutes.

If this statement of the disciplinarian's case sounds harsh and unadorned, think for a moment of the things that visitors to "queer schools" say after the visit is over; and consider whether they do not force the unprejudiced observer to the conclusion that their idea of schools and schooling is just such a harsh and unadorned affair. The discussion of freedom versus authoritative discipline in schools resolves itself after all into a question of the conception of education which is entertained. Are we to believe, with the strict disciplinarian, that education is the process of making a little savage into a little man, that there are many virtues as well as facts that have to be taught to all children so that they may as nearly as possible approach the adult standard? Or are we to believe, with Rousseau, that education is the process of making up the discrepancy between the child at his birth and the man as he will need to be, "that childhood has its own ways of seeing, thinking, and feeling," and that the method of training these ways to what a man will need is to let the child test them upon the world about him?

The phrase, "authoritative discipline," is used purposely, for discipline and freedom are not contradictory ideas. The following quotation from Rousseau shows very plainly what a heavy taskmaster even his freedom was, a freedom so often taken to mean mere lawlessness and license. "Give him [the pupil] no orders at all, absolutely none. Do not even let him think that you claim any authority over him. Let him know only that he is weak and you are strong, that his condition and yours puts him at your mercy; let this be perceived, learned and felt. Let him early find upon his proud neck the heavy yoke which nature has imposed upon us, the heavy yoke of necessity, under which every finite being must bow. Let him find the necessity in things, not in the caprices of man; let the curb be the force of conditions, not authority."

Surely no discipline could be more severe, more apt to develop character and reasonableness, nor less apt to develop disorder and laziness. In fact the real reason for the feeling against freedom in schools seems to come from a misunderstanding. The critic confuses physical liberty with moral and intellectual liberty. Because the pupils are moving about, or sitting on the floor, or have their chairs scattered about instead of in a straight line, because they are using their hands and tongues, the visitor thinks that their minds must be relaxed as well; that they must be simply fooling, with no more restraint for their minds and morals than appears for their bodies. Learning in school has been so long associated with a docile or passive mind that because that useful organ does not squirm or talk in its operations, observers have come to think that none of the child should do so, or it will interfere with learning.

Assuming that educational reformers are right in supposing that the function of education is to help the growing of a helpless young animal into a happy, moral, and efficient human being, a consistent plan of education must allow enough liberty to promote that growth. The child's body must have room to move and stretch itself, to exercise the muscles and to rest when tired. Every one agrees that swaddling clothes are a bad thing for the baby, cramping and interfering with bodily functions. The swaddling clothes of the straight-backed desk, head to the front and hands folded, are just as cramping and even more nerve racking to the school child. It is no wonder that pupils who have to sit in this way for several hours a day break out in bursts of immoderate noise and fooling as soon as restraining influences are removed. Since they do not have a normal outlet for their physical energy to spend itself, it is stored up, and when opportunity offers it breaks forth all the more impetuously because of the nervous irritation previously suffered in repressing the action of an imperfectly trained body. Give a child liberty to move and stretch when he needs it, with opportunities for real exercise all through the day and he will not become so nervously overwrought that he is irritable or aimlessly boisterous when left to himself. Trained in *doing* things, he will be able to keep at work and to think of other people when he is not under restraining supervision.

A truly scientific education can never develop so long as children are treated in the lump, merely as a class. Each child has a strong individuality, and any science must take stock of all the facts in its material. Every pupil must have a chance to show what he truly is, so that the teacher can find out what he needs to make him a complete human being. Only as a teacher becomes acquainted with each one of her pupils can she hope to understand childhood, and it is only as she understands it that she can hope to evolve any scheme of education which shall approach either the scientific or the artistic standard. As long as educators do not know their individual facts they can never know whether their hypotheses are of value. But how are they to know their material if they impose themselves upon it to such an extent that each portion is made to act just like every other portion? If the pupils are marched into line, information presented to them which they are then expected to give back in uniform fashion, nothing will ever be found out about any of them. But if every pupil has an opportunity to express himself, to show what are his particular qualities, the teacher will have material on which to base her plans of instruction.

Since a child lives in a social world, where even the simplest act or word is bound up with the words and acts of his neighbors, there is no danger that this liberty will sacrifice the interests of others to caprice. Liberty does not mean the removal of the checks which nature and man impose on the life of every individual in the community, so that one individual may indulge impulses which go against his own welfare as a member of society. But liberty for the child is the chance to test all impulses and tendencies on the world of things and people in which he finds himself, sufficiently to discover their character so that he may get rid of those which are harmful, and develop those which are useful to himself and others. Education which treats all children as if their impulses were those of the average of an adult society (whose weaknesses and failures are moreover constantly deplored) is sure to go on reproducing that same average society without even finding out whether and how it might be better. Education which finds out what children really are may be able to shape itself by this knowledge so that the best can be kept and the bad eliminated. Meantime much is lost by a mere external suppression of the bad which equally prevents the expression of the better.

If education demands liberty before it can shape itself according to facts, how is it to use this liberty for the benefit of the child? Give a child freedom to find out what he can and can not do, both in the way of what is physically possible and what his neighbors will stand for, and he will not waste much time on impossibilities but will bend his energies to the possibilities. The physical energy and mental inquisitiveness of children can be turned into positive channels. The teacher will find the spontaneity, the liveliness, and initiative of the pupil aids in teaching, instead of being, as under the coercive system, nuisances to be repressed. The very things which are now interferences will become positive qualities that the teacher is cultivating. Besides preserving qualities which will be of use to the man and developing habits of independence and industry, allowing the child this freedom is necessary if pupils are really to learn by doing. Most doing will lead only to superficial muscle training if it is dictated to the child and prescribed for him step by step. But when the child's natural curiosity and love of action are put to work on useful problems, on finding out for himself how to adjust his environment to his needs, the teacher finds that the pupils are not only doing their lessons as well as ever, but are also learning how to control and put to productive use those energies which are simply disturbing in the average classroom. Unless the pupil has some real work on which to exercise his mind by means of his senses and muscles, the teacher will not be able to do away with the ordinary disciplinary methods. For in a classroom where the teacher is doing all the work and the children are listening and answering questions, it would be absurd to allow the children to place themselves where they please, to move about, or to talk. Where the teacher's rôle has changed to that of helper and observer, where the development of every child is the goal, such freedom becomes as much a necessity of the work as is quiet where the children are simply reciting.

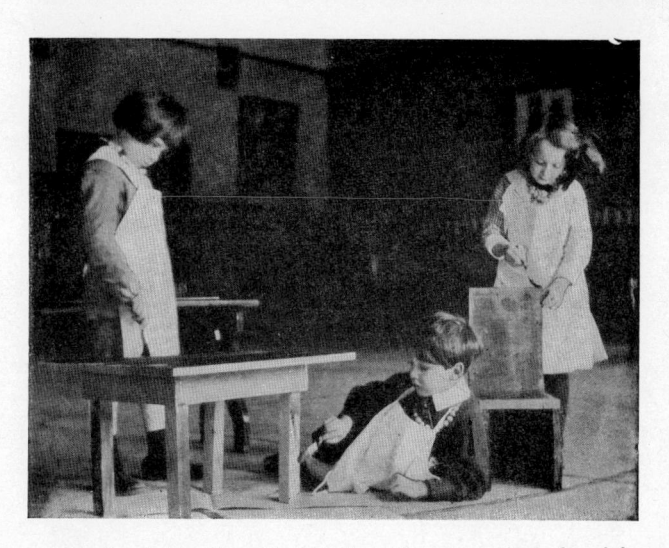

Learning to live through situations that are typical of social life. (Teachers College, N. Y. City.)

FREEDOM AND INDIVIDUALITY 141

At present, the most talked of schools in which freedom and liberty are necessary for the children's work are the schools of Madame Maria Montessori in Italy and those of her pupils in this country. Madame Montessori believes, with many educators in this country, that liberty is necessary in the classroom if the teacher is to know the needs and capabilities of each pupil, if the child is to receive in school a well-rounded training making for the best development of his mind, character, and physique. In general, her reasons for insisting upon this liberty, which is the basis of her method, correspond with those outlined above, with one exception. She holds that liberty is necessary for the child if a scientific education is to be created, because without it data on which to base principles can not be collected; also that it is necessary for the physical welfare of the pupils and for the best development of their characters in training them to be independent. The point of difference between the Italian educator and most reformers in this country lies in their respective views of the value of liberty in the use of material, and this point will be taken up later.

Madame Montessori believes that repressing children physically while they are in school and teaching them habits of mental passivity and docility is mistaking the function of the school and doing the children real harm. Scientific education not only needs freedom for the child in order to collect data, but liberty is its very basis; "liberty is activity," says Madame Montessori in her book called "The Montessori Method." Activity is the basis of life, consequently training children to move and act is training them for life, which is the proper office of the schoolroom. The object of liberty is the best interests of the whole group; this becomes the end of the liberty allowed the children. Everything which does not contribute to it must be suppressed, while the greatest care is taken to foster every action with a useful scope. In order to give the pupils the largest possible scope for such useful activity, they are allowed a very large amount of freedom in the classroom. They may move about, talk to each other, place their tables and chairs where they please, and, what is of more significance, each pupil may choose what work he will do, and may work at one thing as long or as short a time as he wishes. She says, "A room in which all the children move about usefully, intelligently, and voluntarily, without committing any rough or rude act, would seem to me a classroom very well disciplined indeed." Disci-

FREEDOM AND INDIVIDUALITY 143

pline, in short, is ability to do things independently, not submission under restraint.

In order to bring about this active discipline, which allows free scope for any useful work, and at the same time does not stifle the spontaneous impulses of the child, the ordinary methods of discipline are done away with, and a technique is developed to emphasize the positive, not the negative, side of discipline. Montessori has described it in this way: "As to punishments, we have many times come in contact with children who disturbed the others, without paying any attention to our corrections. Such children were at once examined by the physician. When the case proved to be that of a normal child, we placed one of the little tables in a corner of the room, and in this way isolated the child, having him sit in a comfortable little armchair, so placed that he might see his companions at work, and giving him those games and toys to which he was most attracted. This isolation almost always succeeded in calming the child; from his position he could see the entire assembly of his companions, and the way in which they carried on their work was an object-lesson much more efficacious than any words of the teacher could possibly have been. Little by little he would come to see the advantages of being one of the company working so busily before his eyes, and he would really wish to go back and do as the others did." The corrections which the teachers first offer never take the form of scoldings; the child is quietly told that what he is doing is not polite or disturbs the other children. Then he is told how he ought to behave to be a pleasant companion, or his attention is diverted to a piece of work. Because children are working on something of their own choice, and when they want to, and because they may move and talk enough so that they do not get nervously tired, there is very little need for any "punishment." Except for an isolated case of real lawlessness, such as Montessori refers to in the quotation just cited, the visitor to one of her schools sees very little need of negative discipline. The teachers' corrections are practically all for small breaches of manners or for carelessness.

Activity founded on liberty being the guiding principle of the Montessori schools, activity is expended by the child on two sorts of material. Montessori believes that the child needs practice in the actions of daily life; that, for example, he should be taught how to take care of and wait on himself. Part of the work is accordingly directed to this end. She also believes that the child possesses innate faculties which should be allowed to develop to their fullest; consequently part of the work is designed to give adequate expression to these faculties. These exercises for the culture of the inner potentialities of the child she considers the more important of the two. The child needs to know how to adjust himself to his environment in order to be independent and happy; but an imperfect development of the child's faculties is an imperfect development of life itself; so the real object of education consists in furnishing active help to the normal expansion of the life of the child. These two lines of development Madame Montessori considers to be so distinct one from the other that the exercises of practical life cannot perform the function of the exercises arranged to train the faculties and senses of the child.

The exercises of practical life are designed to teach the child to be independent, to supply his own wants, and to perform the actions of daily life with skill and grace. The pupils keep the schoolroom in order, dusting and arranging the furniture, and putting away each piece of material as soon as they are through with it. They wait on themselves while they are working, getting out the things they want, finding a con-

venient place to work, and then taking care of
the apparatus when they have worked with it as
long as they like. In schools where the children do not live in the building, a midday lunch
is served for the pupils; and, except for the
cooking, the children do all the work connected
with the meal, setting tables, serving food, and
then clearing away and washing the dishes. All
the pupils share alike in this work, regardless
of their age; children of three and four soon
learn to handle the plates and glasses, and to
pass the food. Wherever possible the schools
have gardens, which the children care for, and
animal pets of a useful sort—hens and chickens
or pigeons. Even the youngest children put on
their own wraps, button and unbutton their
aprons and slippers, and when they can not do
it for themselves, they help each other. The
necessity of the pupils' learning to take care of
themselves as early as possible is so much insisted upon that in order to help the youngest
in learning this lesson, Montessori has designed
several appliances to give them practice before
they begin to wait upon themselves. These are
wooden frames, fitted with cloth which is opened
down the center. Then the edges are joined
either with buttons, hooks and eyes, or ribbons,
and practice consists in opening and closing

FREEDOM AND INDIVIDUALITY 147

these edges by buttoning, hooking, or tying as the case may be.

These appliances may be taken as a bridge between the two sorts of exercises in use in the Montessori schools. They mark a transition from the principles which are common to most educational reformers to those associated particularly with the method worked out by Madame Montessori. Another quotation from her first book gives the clew to an understanding of this method: "In a pedagogical method which is experimental the education of the senses must undoubtedly assume the greatest importance. . . . The method used by me is that of making a pedagogical experiment with a didactic object and awaiting the spontaneous reaction of the child. . . . With little children, we must proceed to the making of trials, and must select the didactic materials in which they show themselves to be interested. . . . I believe, however, that I have arrived at a selection of objects representing the minimum necessary to a practical sense education."

Madame Montessori started her career as a teacher among deficient children in the hospitals where Seguin had worked. Naturally she experimented with the material used with her subnormal pupils when she began working with normal children. It is equally natural that many of the objects which had proved useful with the former were also usable with the average school child. Ordinary school methods succeed with deficient children when used more slowly and with more patience; and in the same way Madame Montessori found that many of the appliances which had before been used only for deficients produced remarkably successful results with ordinary children, when used with more rapidity and liberty. Therefore her "didactic material" includes many things that are used generally to develop sensory consciousness among deficients. But instead of using the material in a fixed order and under the guidance of a teacher, the normal child is allowed complete liberty in its use; for the object is no longer to awaken powers that are nearly lacking, but to exercise powers that the child is using constantly in all his daily actions, so that he may have a more and more accurate and skillful control over them.

The exercises to develop the faculties of the child are especially so arranged as to train the power to discriminate and to compare. His sensory organs are nearly all exercised with apparatus designed, like the button frames, to allow the child to do one thing for one purpose.

FREEDOM AND INDIVIDUALITY 149

The pupil does not have to use these objects in any fixed order or work for any length of time on one thing. Except for the very youngest children, who do only the very simplest exercises, pupils are at liberty to work at any one they wish and for as long as they wish. Montessori believes that the child will turn naturally to the exercise he is ready for. The materials to develop the sense of touch are among the simplest. There are small boards with strips of sandpaper running from the roughest to the smoothest, and pieces of different kinds of cloth; these the child rubs his hands over while his eyes are blindfolded, distinguishing the differences. The appliances designed to teach the child to distinguish differences of form and size use the sense of touch as a strong aid to sight. There are blocks of wood with holes of different diameters and depths, and cylinders to fit each hole. The child takes all the cylinders out, rubs his fingers around their edge and then around the rim of the holes and puts them back in the proper hole. The ability to judge of size is also exercised by giving the child a set of graduated wooden blocks with which he builds a tower, and another set which he may use to make a stair. The power to distinguish form is developed by wooden insets of all shapes which fit into holes in a thin board. The child takes out the insets, feels of them and then replaces them. Later the teacher tells him the geometrical name of each form while he is touching it, and then has him distinguish them by name.

There are sets of cardboard forms to correspond to the wooden ones, and metal plaques where the form appears as a hole in the center of the plaque. These are used in games which consist in matching the same form in the different materials, and for drawing the form in outline on paper to be filled in with colored pencils.

The method of teaching reading and writing uses the sense of touch to reënforce the lesson the pupil gets through the eye and ear. Sandpaper alphabets with each letter pasted on a square of cardboard are given a child. He rubs his finger over these as if he were writing and makes the sound of the letter as he rubs. Movable letters are used only after the child is familiar with the letters by touch, and with them he makes words. Writing usually precedes reading when children learn in this way; when they take pencil or chalk, they are able to trace the letters with very little difficulty because the muscles as well as the eye are familiar with the forms.

FREEDOM AND INDIVIDUALITY 151

The sense of hearing is exercised by means of two sets of bells, one fixed to give the scale, the other movable, so that the child can make his own scale by comparing with the fixed scale. The children play a number of games where they are as quiet as possible, acting out simple, whispered directions from the teacher. There is as well a series of rattles filled with sand, gravel, and grains, and the game is to guess which rattle is being shaken. The sense of color is developed in the same way by means of specially arranged apparatus. This consists of small tablets wound with colored silks in all colors and shades, which are used in many different ways, according to the age and skill of the pupil. The youngest learn to distinguish two or three colors and to tell dark from light shades. The older pupils who are familiar with the colors acquire enough skill in their manipulation to be able to glance at one tablet and then go to the other side of the room and bring either an exact match or the next shade lighter or darker, according to what the teacher has asked for.

Muscular development is provided for by giving the children plenty of time during the school day to run and play, and by means of apparatus for free gymnastics, while the finer coördinating muscles are being constantly exercised while the child is manipulating the appliances for sense training. The faculty of speech is trained by having the children practice the pronunciation of words and syllables. The fundamental conceptions of number are taught much as are reading and writing. Besides the sandpaper numbers and the plain cardboard ones, there is a series of wooden bars varying in length from one to ten meters, which the children use in connection with numbers in learning the combinations up to ten.

The foregoing description of the didactic material is very brief and general and omits many of the uses of the appliances as well as reference to some of the less used material, but it serves to illustrate the nature and purpose of the work done by the children. Pupils acquire a marked skill in the handling of the material which appeals especially to them, and children of four and five learn to write with very little effort, In fact, Madame Montessori believes that the average child is ready for many of the ideas which he usually does not get until his sixth year at an earlier age, when they can be acquired more easily; and that a system such as hers which allows the child to perform one set of acts at the time when he is ready for it saves him

FREEDOM AND INDIVIDUALITY 153

a great deal of time later on, besides giving a more perfect result than could then be achieved.

Each piece of material is designed to train singly one specific sense through the performance of one set of fixed acts. Consequently if liberty is confounded with doing as one pleases, this method must appear very strict. Liberty is found in the use the children make of the material. The amount of freedom the pupils are allowed in the classroom has already been described, and the rôle of the teacher is made to correspond with this liberty. She is trained not to interfere with any spontaneous activity of the child and never to force his attention where it is not given naturally. When a child has turned of his own accord to a certain apparatus the teacher may show him the proper use of it; or in rare cases she may try to direct the child's attention to a different type of work if he seems inclined to concentrate to excess on one thing, but if she fails she never insists. In fact nothing is done by the teacher to call the child's attention to his weaknesses and failures, or to arouse any negative associations in his mind. Madame Montessori says, "If he [the child] makes a mistake, the teacher must not correct him, but must suspend her lesson to take it up again another day. Indeed, why correct him? If the child has not succeeded in associating the name with the object, the only way in which to succeed would be to repeat both the action of the sense stimuli and the name; in others words, to repeat the lesson. But when the child has failed, we should know that he was not at that instant ready for the physic associations which we wished to provoke in him, and we must therefore choose another moment. If we should say, in correcting the child, 'No, you have made a mistake,' all these words, which, being in the form of a reproof, would strike him more forcibly than others, would remain in the mind of the child, retarding the learning of the names. On the contrary, the silence which follows the error leaves the field of consciousness clear, and the next lesson may successfully follow the first.''

The simplicity and passivity of the teachers' rôle are increased by the nature of the didactic material. Once the child has been taught the nomenclature connected with the apparatus, the teacher ceases to teach. She becomes merely an observer as far as that pupil is concerned until he is ready to move on to another appliance. This is possible because of what Montessori calls the "self-corrective" nature of her material. That is, each thing is arranged so that

FREEDOM AND INDIVIDUALITY

the child can do but one complete thing with it, so that if he makes a mistake the apparatus does not work. Thus a child working with any one thing does not have to be told when he makes a mistake how to correct it. He is confronted with an obvious problem, which is solved by his own handling of the material. The child is educating himself in that he sees his own mistakes and corrects them, and the finished result is perfect; partial success or failure is not possible.

Take the simplest piece of material, the block of wood in which solid cylinders are set. There are ten of these cylinders, each varying, say, in length about a quarter of an inch from the one next it. The child takes all these cylinders from their proper holes and mixes them up; then he puts them back in their right places again. If he puts a cylinder in a hole too deep for it, it disappears; if the hole is too shallow it sticks up too far, while if every cylinder is put in its proper hole, the child has a solid block of wood again. All the geometrical insets are self-corrective in exactly the same way. Even the youngest child would know whether he had succeeded with the button and lacing frames. The tower blocks will not pile up into a tower unless the child piles them one on top of the other in decreasing sizes, nor will the stair blocks make a stair unless they are laid side by side according to the same principle. In using the color tablets the child needs rather more preparation; but when he has learned to distinguish the eight different shades of one of the eight colors, he is ready to arrange them so that they blend from dark to light, and if he makes a mistake the tablet placed in wrong sequence will appear to him as an inharmonious blot. Once the pupil gets the idea with one color he is able to work it out for himself for the other seven. Since the pupils are never allowed merely to play with an apparatus, it becomes associated in his mind with performing the right set of actions, so a misstep appears to him as something to be undone, something calling for another trial. The educational purpose Montessori aims to serve in making her material self-corrective, is that of leading the child to concentrate upon the differences in the parts of the appliances he is working with; that is, in trying for the fixed end he has to compare and discriminate between two colors, two sounds, two dimensions, etc. It is in making these comparisons that the intellectual value of training the senses lies. The particular faculty or sense that the child is exercising in using any one apparatus is sharpened by concentration upon the *relations* between the things. Sense-development of an intellectual character comes from the growth of this power of the sense organ to compare and discriminate, not from teaching the child to recognize dimensions, sounds, colors, etc., nor yet from simply going through certain motions without making a mistake. Montessori claims that intellectual result differentiates her work from the appliances of the kindergarten.

As we said above, the difference between the Montessori method and the views of American reformers lies not in a difference of opinion as to the value of liberty, but rather in a different conception of the best use to be made of it. Physically the pupils of a Montessori class are freer than they are in the classes of most American educators with whose views this book has been dealing; intellectually they are not so free. They can come and go, work and be idle, talk and move about quite voluntarily; getting information about things and acquiring skill in movement are the ends secured. Each pupil works independently on material that is self-corrective. But there is no freedom allowed the child to create. He is free to choose which apparatus he will use, but never to choose his own ends, never to bend a material to his own plans. For the material is limited to a fixed number of things which must be handled in a certain way. Most American educators think that the training of the pupil to habits of right thinking and judgment is best accomplished by means of material which presents to him real problems, and they think that the measure of reality is found in connection with the experiences of life out of school. The big thing that children have to learn is twofold; for their adjustment to the world in which they find themselves involves relations to people and to things. Adjustment means not simply the ability to control their bodies, but an intellectual adjustment as well, an ability to see the relations between things, to look behind their surface and perceive their meaning not alone to the individual, but to the community as well. "The best way of making sure that children learn this double adjustment is," says the American school-teacher, "to give them work which represents truly the conditions they have to deal with out of school."

Outside the classroom the child is constantly having to bend material things to his own needs, and to satisfy the demands that are made upon him because he lives with other people. If he is to accomplish this successfully for himself

Solving problems in school as they would have to be met out of school. (Francis Parker School, Chicago.)

and others it is important that he learn to see things as they are; that he be able to use his senses accurately to understand the meaning that things and people have to and for him as a member of society. Hence the need of freedom to meet and solve these problems in school, much as one has to do out of school. Madame Montessori, on the other hand, believes that the technique of living can best be learned by the child through situations that are not typical of social life, but which have been arranged in order to exercise some special sense so as to develop the faculties of discrimination and comparison.

The difference of opinion resolves itself into the acceptance of different views of the nature of the human intelligence. Montessori, in common with the older psychologists, believes that people have ready-made faculties which can be trained and developed for general purposes, regardless of whether the acts by which they are exercised have any meaning other than the training they afford. The child is born with undeveloped faculties which can be made to blossom by suitable appliances, and then devoted at will to other uses. Most educators in this country agree with the newer psychological theories that skill can not be achieved independently of the tools used and the object fashioned in the accomplishment of a special end. Exercises which distinguish for the child the abstract qualities like length and color, regardless of the things of which they are qualities, may give the child great skill in performing the special exercise, but will not necessarily result in making him more successful in dealing with these qualities as they appear as factors in the situations of life. Much less will they train powers of comparing and discriminating at large so that they may be transferred to any use. A child is not born with faculties to be unfolded, but with special impulses of action to be developed through their use in preserving and perfecting life in the social and physical conditions under which it goes on.

If, accordingly, the child in an American progressive school does not usually have as much freedom of moving about and of choice of his time for doing work, the explanation does not consist in a less degree of belief in the value of liberty. The emphasis falls on the larger freedom of using and testing senses and judgment in situations typical of life. Because these situations are social, they require that children work more together in common pursuits; because they are social they permit and often require the teacher's aid, just as one gains assistance from others in the ordinary affairs of life. Help from others is not to be feared as an encroachment upon liberty, but that kind of help which restricts the use of the children's own intelligence in forming ends and using ingenuity, initiative and inventiveness in the selection and adaption of materials. The limitation of material to performing exercises calculated to train an isolated sense—a situation that never presents itself in life—seems to the American teacher a greater limitation of freedom than that which arises from the need of coöperation with others in the performance of common activities. It is desirable not merely that the child should learn not to interfere with others as they execute their own ends, but also that he should learn to work with them in an intelligent way. Hence the scope of the material should not be limited to training the discriminations and comparisons of a single sense (however valuable this may be with very young children who are incapable of coöperative activity and whose main business is to master the use of their organs),* but should be varied enough to offer typical problems call-

* It is significant that many who have experimented with the apparatus hold that its value is greatest with quite young children—three and four years old.

ing for the kind of comparison and discrimination used in ordinary life-situations. And when pupils are making real things for real uses, or finding out about the activities and materials of out-of-school life, several children need to work at the same thing and keep at one thing with some consecutiveness.

But if the educators of this country differ with Montessori as to the existence of innate faculties which can be trained for general application by special exercises designed only for training and not for the accomplishment of results in which training is incidental, they welcome her efforts to secure that degree of freedom in the schoolroom which will enable teachers to become acquainted with the real powers and interests of the child and thus secure the data for a scientific method in education. They appreciate the force of her point that artificial conditions of restraint prevent teachers from getting true knowledge of the material with which they are dealing, so that instruction is limited to repetition of traditional processes. They perceive that her insistence upon touch associated with muscular movement as a factor in learning to write and read, is a real contribution to the technique of elementary instruction. She has become a most important factor in the popularizing of the gospel of liberty as indispensable to any true education.

With a wider understanding of the meaning of intellectual and moral freedom, and the accompanying breakdown of the negative and coercive ideas of discipline, the chief obstacle to the use of the teacher's own powers of observation and experimentation will disappear. The scientific interest which requires personal observation, reflection, and experimental activity, will be added to the teacher's sympathetic interest in the welfare of children. Education that associates learning with doing will replace the passive education of imparting the learning of others. However well the latter is adapted to feudal societies, in which most individuals are expected to submit constantly and docilely to the authority of superiors, an education which proceeds on this basis is inconsistent with a democratic society where initiative and independence are the rule and where every citizen is supposed to take part in the conduct of affairs of common interest. It is significant of the wide-reaching development of the democratic spirit that the voice most influentially identified at the present time with the ideal of liberty in education should sound forth from Italy.

CHAPTER VII

THE RELATION OF THE SCHOOL TO THE COMMUNITY

WORK is essentially social in its character, for the occupations which people carry on are for human needs and ends. They are concerned with maintaining the relations with things and with others which make up the world we live in. Even the acts that are concerned with keeping alive are arranged to fit into a social scheme which has modified all man's instinctive acts and thoughts. Everything about this scheme is dependent upon the ability of people to work together successfully. If they can do this a well-balanced, happy and prosperous society results. Without these occupations, which are essentially social life—that is human life— civilization can not go on. The result is a sort of social education by necessity, since every one must learn to adapt himself to other individuals and to whole communities. When it is left to circumstances this education, although necessary, is haphazard and only partial. We send children to school supposedly to learn in a systematic way the occupations which constitute living, but to a very large extent the schools overlook, in the methods and subject-matter of their teaching, the social basis of living. Instead of centering the work in the concrete, the human side of things, they put the emphasis on the abstract, hence the work is made academic—unsocial. Work then is no longer connected with a group of people all engaged in occupations, but is isolated, selfish and individualistic. It is based on a conception of society which no longer fits the facts, an every-man-for-himself society which ceased to exist a hundred years ago. The ordinary school curriculum ignores the scientific democratic society of to-day and its needs and ideals, and goes on fitting children for an individualistic struggle for existence, softened by a little intellectual "culture" for the individual's enjoyment.

Schools started in this country in pioneer days, when a comparatively small number of people were scattered over an immense country that offered them unlimited and unexplored opportunities. The pioneer was dependent upon his own ability in seizing these opportunities, in getting ahead, in his use of nature's raw material. He lived much alone and for himself; no one was really dependent upon his relations with others; for there were few people, endless material, and unorganized communities, without traditions or institutions. The welfare of the country was dependent upon the spread of the doctrines of getting on, and every man for himself. It was entirely natural that the new schools should reflect this ideal and shape their work to drive home the lesson. Our early settlers came from countries with traditions of culture and "learning"; and it was natural that they should look to their schools to keep alive these transplanted ideals in the midst of their struggle with nature. Culture did not mean to them a harmonious development of all the child's faculties, but it meant rather the storing up of historical facts and the acquiring of knowledge and the literatures of the past. Learning, too, did not mean finding out about the things around them or about what was going on in other parts of the world; it meant reviewing the achievements of the past, learning to read the dead languages, the deader the language the greater the reputation for "learning." The school curriculums were principally devoted, therefore, to turning the eyes of the pupils to the past, where alone they could find things worth studying and where, too, they might find the refinements of esthetic and intellectual development. A knowledge of the "three R's" and a little natural "smartness" was all the social equipment the child needed, all the preparation that was necessary for him to begin to get on in the world. Once he had that equipment the schools could then turn their attention to giving him culture.

However interesting or enlightening such culture might be to the individual, obviously the first business of the public school is to teach the child to live in the world in which he finds himself, to understand his share in it, and to get a good start in adjusting himself to it. Only as he can do these things successfully will he have time or inclination to cultivate purely intellectual activities.

The public schools started with the awakening of the spirit of liberty and democracy. More and more people realized that there was no possibility of an equal chance for every one, if a very small minority of the population had entire control of the material of science, which was so rapidly changing all social and industrial conditions. Naturally enough when these popular schools were started, the community turned to the schools already in existence for their curriculum and organization. The old schools, however, were not conducted to give equal opportunity to all, but for just the opposite purpose, to make more marked the line between classes, to give the leisure and moneyed classes something which every one could not get, to cater to their desire for distinction and to give them occupation.

People lived generation after generation in the same place, carrying on the same occupations under the same conditions. Their world was so small that it did not seem to offer much in the way of material for a school education; and what it did offer was primarily concerned with earning a living. But the schools were for people who did not earn their own livings, for people who wished to be accomplished, polished and interesting socially, so the material was abstract, purposely separated from the concrete and the useful. Ideals of culture and education were and still are to a surprising extent based entirely upon the interests and demands of an aristocratic and leisure class. Having such an ideal of culture it was natural to the pioneers to copy the curriculum of the schools made for this ideal, even when the purpose of their schools was to give an equal industrial and social chance to all. From the very beginning of the public schools in this country the material of the curriculum reflected social conditions which were rapidly passing away: ideals of education that a feudal society, dependent upon its aristocracy, had developed.

The tremendous change in society which the application of science to industry brought about, changes which caused the French Revolution and the general revolution of 1848, effected a reconstruction of nearly all the institutions of civilization, the death of a great many, and the birth of many more. The need of popular education was one of the results of the change, and with this need came the public schools. As their form did not adapt itself to the new conditions, but simply copied the schools already existing, the process of reconstruction to fit the new society is still going on, and is only just beginning to become conscious. A democratic society, dependent upon applications of science for all its prosperity and welfare, can not hope to use with any great success a system of education which grew up for the ruling body in an autocratic society using only human power for its industries and wealth. The ever-increasing dissatisfaction with the schools and the experiments in trade and industrial training which are being started, are protests against clinging to this outworn inheritance. They are the first steps in the process of building a new education which shall really give an equal chance to every one, because it will base itself on the world in which the children live.

There are three things about the old-fashioned school which must be changed if schools are to reflect modern society: first, the subject-matter, second, the way the teacher handles it, and third, the way the pupils handle it. The subject-matter will not be altered as to name. Reading, writing, arithmetic and geography will always be needed, but their substance will be greatly altered and added to. In the first place modern society realizes that the care and growth of the body are just as important as the development of the mind; more so, for the latter is dependent upon the former, so schools will become places for children to learn to live physically as well as mentally. Again we need to know how to read and write nowadays so that we may be able to do the simplest daily actions, take the right street-car, avoid dangerous places, and keep in touch with people and events we can not see, and, in fact, do almost everything connected with our occupations. But the schools are still teaching reading and writing as if they were ends in themselves, simply luxuries to be acquired by pupils for their private edification. The same thing is true of geography; pupils learn boundaries, populations and rivers as if their object was to store up facts that everybody may not know. But in a society where railroads and steamboats, newspapers and telegraph, have made the whole world neighbors, and where no community is self-supporting, the desirability of really knowing about these neighbors is obvious. In other words our world has been so tremendously enlarged and complicated, our horizons so widened and our sympathies so stimulated, by the changes in our surroundings and habits brought about by machinery, that a school curriculum which does not show this same growth can be only very partially successful. The subject-matter of the schoolroom must be enlarged to take in the new elements and needs of society. This can be done without overburdening the pupils by effecting the second and third necessary changes.

The complication and multiplication due to machinery and the increase in the mere number of facts that are known about things through scientific discoveries, make the task of mastering even one subject almost impossible. When we consider all the facts connected with teaching the geography of our own country, the climatic and geological facts, the racial facts, the industrial and political facts, and the social and scientific facts, we begin to realize the hopelessness of teaching with lists of facts. Geography embraces nearly the entire range of human knowledge and endeavor. The same thing is true to a lesser extent of all the subjects in the curriculum. The great number of facts at our disposal in any one branch makes a mere classification of the principal ones seem like a makeshift. So teachers, instead of having their classes read and then recite facts from textbooks, must change their methods. Facts present themselves to every one in countless numbers, and it is not their naming that is useful, but the ability to understand them and see their relation and application to each other. So the function of the teacher must change from that of a cicerone and dictator to that of a watcher and helper. As teachers come to watch their individual pupils with a view to allowing each one the fullest development of his thinking and reasoning powers, and to use the tables of reading, writing, and arithmetic as means of training the child's abilities to judge and act, the rôle of the child necessarily changes too. It becomes active instead of passive, the child becomes the questioner and experimenter.

It is the rare mind that can get relations or draw conclusions from simply hearing facts. Most people must see and handle things before they can tell how these things will behave and what their meaning is. The teacher then becomes the one who sees that the pupils get proper material, and that they use it in ways that are true; that is, in ways that represent relations and conditions that actually exist outside the classroom. This is simply another way of saying that in a society where every one is supposed to take care of himself, and is supposed to have liberty of person and action, up to the point of harming others, it is pretty important that every one should be able to conduct himself, that is, to act so that he can take care of himself successfully. For its own sake society can not afford to train up its children in a way that blunts and dulls the quickness and accuracy of judgment of the baby before it begins school. If it does this it is increasing the number of incompetents who will be a drag on the whole of society. Dogmatic methods which prescribe and make for docility and passivity not only become ineffective in modern society but they actually hinder the development of the largest possibilities of society.

All the educational reformers following Rousseau have looked to education as the best means of regenerating society. They have been fighting against the feudal and pioneer notion that the reason for a good education was to enable your children and mine to get ahead of the rest of the community, to give individuals another weapon to use in making society contribute more to their purse and pleasure. They have believed that the real reason for developing the best possible education was to prevent just this, by developing methods which would give a harmonious development of all the powers. This can be done by socializing education, by making schools a real part of active life, not by allowing them to go their own way, shunting off all outside influences, and isolating themselves. Froebel, Pestalozzi, and their followers tried to effect just this linking up with society which would result in the development of a social spirit in every one. But they did not have the means for making their schools embryo communities. The demand for popular education was still so small that the community was not willing to recognize the schools as an integral part, and the idea that children were anything but miniature grown-ups, was still so new that successful methods of handling groups of children had not been developed. The rôle of the community in making the schools vital is just as important as the rôle of the school itself. For in a community where schools are looked upon as isolated institutions, as a necessary convention, the school will remain largely so in spite of the most skillful methods of teaching. But a community that demands something visible from its schools, that recognizes the part they play in the welfare of the whole just as it recognizes its police and fire departments, that uses the energies and interest of its youthful citizens, not simply controlling their time until they are prepared to be turned out as citizens—such a community will have social schools, and whatever its resources, it will have schools that develop community spirit and interests.

A great deal has been written lately about the public school system at Gary, Ind., with special reference to the novel features of school administration that are being worked out there, or else with emphasis on the opportunities for industrial training. But the biggest idea there is the one behind these new features. It is the social and community idea. Mr. Wirt, the superintendent of schools, has had an opportunity to make the schools of the steel town almost from the very beginning of the town, and he has wanted to do it right. He did not visit the most famous schools all over the country or send for the best school architect; instead he stayed right at home, and forgetting what had or had not been done in other places, he tried to make the best possible schools for Gary. The question he tried to answer was this: What did the Gary children need to make them good citizens and happy and prosperous human beings, and how could the money available for educational purposes supply all these needs? The industrial features of his schools will be taken up later, but it may be well to point out in passing that they were not instituted to turn out good workers for the steel company, nor to save the factories the expense of training their own workers, but for the educational value of the work they involved. In the same way it would be a mistake to consider the Gary schools simply as an attempt to take the unpromising immigrant child and turn him into a self-supporting immigrant, or as an attempt to meet the demand of an industrial class for a certain sort of training.

Mr. Wirt found himself the superintendent of schools in an American town, responsible for thousands of children coming from all sorts of surroundings. It was his problem to take care

The pupil stays in the same building from day nursery through high school. (Gary, Ind.)

of them for a number of years in such a way that at the end of the time each child would be able to find his own job and do it successfully, whether this was feeding a machine or managing a business, whether it was taking care of a family or working in an office, or teaching school. His problem is not to give the special information each one may need for the details of his work, but to keep the natural interests and enthusiasms of childhood, to enable each pupil to gain control of his mind and body, and to insure his being able to do the rest for himself. To be successful as a human being and an American citizen, is the goal that the public schools of the country have set for their pupils: earning a living forms part of this ideal, and follows as a matter of course if the larger training is successful. There are many factors to be considered in deciding on the best ways of reaching this goal: such as the individual peculiarities of every child that goes to school; the people that will teach; the neighborhood in which the child lives; and the larger community which pays for the schools. Mr. Wirt's plan takes advantage to their full value of the contributions each one has to make to the whole scheme. Each factor is a contributory asset; without it the others could not perform their work; therefore it means a weak spot in the result if anything is overlooked.

A tremendous waste in the organization of the ordinary public school appears at the first glance to a critic who is seeking to spend the school taxes with the greatest possible benefit to the children and to the taxpayers. The entire school equipment of building, yard, and supplies stands empty for half of every school day, besides summer vacation and Saturdays. The buildings are expensive and for the greater part of the time are not in use at all. This is an extravagance in itself, but when we consider the way the average child who goes to public school in town or city spends the hours when he is not in school, and the very incomplete education he gets during the school hours, we begin to realize just how serious this extravagance is. Mr. Wirt decided to keep the schools open all day in Gary, so that the children would not be forced to spend the greater part of their time playing in the alleys and on crowded street corners, exposed to all the dangers to health and morals that such places offer for the loiterer. Still the buildings would be closed for many hours a day and for many weeks, and he decided that the people who built the buildings—the tax-payers

—ought to have a chance to use them for public purposes during this time, so the Gary schools have evening school, Saturday classes, and summer sessions. This makes the up-keep of the buildings much more expensive than having them open for a few months only, therefore some way of running the plant more economically must be discovered.

Children can not sit still all day at their desks as they do for five hours in most schools; therefore other things must be provided for them to do if they are to keep well and busy during eight hours of school. The Gary buildings obtain this necessary economy by using a building for twice as many pupils as the ordinary building is supposed to be able to take care of. There are two schools in every house, one from eight to three and the other from nine to four, and each takes its turn at the regular classrooms during alternate hours, the remaining half of the day being spent in the various occupations that make Gary unique. In this way enough money is saved to equip shops and pay extra teachers for the subjects that supplement the regular curriculum, and to pay for the extra sessions. Thus with taxes of ordinary size the people of Gary get schools that utilize the children's time, and give them greatly increased facilities for learning, besides offering the adults of the community opportunities for special courses in evening school. At present in Gary the number of adults using the school buildings is greater than the number of children, though of course the number of hours they attend school is much shorter. By having two duplicate schools in every building one half the usual cost per classroom is saved, and enough money to supply healthy activities for the children for eight hours a day and to keep the schools open evenings, holidays and Sundays for adults is obtained.

Each building is equipped with a gymnasium, swimming pool, and playground, and has physical directors that are in attendance for the entire eight hours. Physical training is as much a part of the regular school work as anything else, and besides the work that is part of every pupil's program there are two hours a day when the playground is open for the children to use as they please. Instead of going to the streets to play, the children stay in the school and use the play opportunities it offers. For the most part the physical training takes the form of supervised play and apparatus work. Experimentation has shown here as in so many other places that the pupils are not really interested in the formal group exercises, and that they go through with them under compulsion and so lose most of the benefit. So for the gymnastic drill, swimming pool, tennis courts, and apparatus are largely substituted. The directors see that the individual gets the special exercise that he needs so that the work does not lose its orderliness or effectiveness, and besides getting physical development suited to his needs, every child has a healthy and pleasant place to play or otherwise spend his time outdoors.

The Gary pupil is expected to gain physically during the school year just as he is expected to keep up with his grade in his other work. Each child is examined by a doctor, and the pupils who are not strong enough for the strain of the classroom work are not sent home to do nothing until they are stronger, but are kept in school and given a program suited to their strength, their classroom time is cut down to a minimum, and they spend most of the day on the playground or in the gymnasium, doing the sort of things the doctor says they need to get strong. The physical growth of the pupils is just as important as the mental, and by devoting the same care to it that is given to the child's progress through the grades, the schools go a long way towards making themselves a small community which gives every opportunity for a normal and natural life.

The schools are open eight hours a day, but the grade teachers teach for only six hours, while the physical directors are on duty for the whole time. Four hours of each school's time is given to the regular classroom work or laboratories, and one hour for the auditorium and one hour for "application" or play. Then there are the other two hours when the children may use the play facilities if they wish, and they all do use them. By rotating the classes the number of teachers does not have to be increased, and the pupils get the benefit of teachers especially trained for the subject they are teaching. By dividing each school into groups of pupils the classes are smaller than in most public schools. For the first two hours in the morning—from 8:15 to 10:15—one school has the use of the classrooms, studios, shops and laboratories, one group in a recitation room for the first hour and in the shops for the second, the second group beginning with the shop work. The other school uses the playground for the first hour and attendance is not compulsory, for the second hour one group goes to the auditorium and the other remains on the playground for systematic gymnastics or has an "application'' period. Then at 10:15 the first school goes to the auditorium and playgrounds for its work and the second school takes possession of the class and shop rooms for two hours. Grades one to five have two hours daily in regular classrooms for formal instruction in language, history, literature, and mathematics. Grades six to twelve have three hours daily for this formal instruction. The additional hour is taken from the play and application periods. Grades one to five have one hour of laboratory work in science or shop work in industrial training, thirty minutes for music or literature, and thirty minutes for physical training. Grades six to twelve have the entire two hours for shop work in industrial training, laboratory work in science, or music and drawing.

By this scheme of alternation of classes and schools twice the number of children that are usually cared for in one building are taken care of in smaller classes by teachers who are specialists in their subjects. For besides the industrial teachers, there are teachers for French, German, history, mathematics, literature, music, art, nature study, and the sciences. This additional efficiency is paid for by the saving on buildings effected by the two school systems. Each grade room is used by at least four different classes, so each child does not have a desk where he keeps his things and belongings, but has a locker for his books and changes his classroom at the end of the hour. No one teacher is responsible for one set of pupils, but for her own work, and in the same way the pupils are responsible for themselves. Obviously such a scheme as this requires a real spirit of coöperation among the pupils and teachers, and also good business management.

Mr. Wirt believes that lack of just this has been one of the reasons why the public schools have lost so many of the opportunities that Gary is using. Running a big institution successfully from the business end is a large order in itself, and Mr. Wirt feels that school principals and supervisors have been too greatly handicapped in being expected to do this business while carrying out an educational program. He believes that the school principal or superintendent should be a business manager, an administrative officer simply for the building or for the city. The educational policy of the schools, the program, and methods should be looked out for by experts who are free from the details of administration. These supervising educators should not be appointed for districts but for subjects, and should move their offices from time to time from one school to another, so that they may really keep in touch with all the work in their subject, and so that no one school will be overstrong in one subject. These supervisors should act as the educational principals of the schools where they have their offices for the time, and the whole body of supervisors arrange the curricula for all the schools. Gary has too few schools as yet to enable the completion of such a plan, but the present organization shows the same broad-mindedness and desire to get the coöperation and value of all the work of all the teachers through the system, from the newest assistant to the superintendent himself.

In discipline, in social life, and in the curriculum the Gary schools are doing everything possible, in coöperation with church and home, to use to the best educational purpose every resource of money, organization and neighborhood influence. The school is a small community in its discipline, and a democratic one. The work is so well arranged that the children want to go to school; there is no need to drag them with truant officers or overawe them by a show of stern authority. Once in the school building they feel at home and take the same interest and responsibility in the work that they take in their own homes. Each child knows what all the other children and classes are doing, for all the children are constantly meeting in the locker rooms or as they pass through the halls for their change of classroom at the end of every hour. The auditorium and the system of visiting classes, and the repairing and manufacturing of school equipment by the students, are strong factors in creating the spirit that prevails among the scholars. There is a student council in each school elected by the students to attend to the interests of the student body and to the order of the building. There are health campaigns carried on by the school doctors coöperating through the school printing press with the English classes and the auditorium periods. The children take such a keen interest in these, and work so hard that there is a larger percent. of contagious diseases among the children under school age than among those in school, in spite of the greater chances for contagion among the latter. Instead of simply enforcing the health laws, the school authorities tell the children what the laws are, why they were made and how they can help to keep down contagion and all sorts of sickness; in chemistry and cooking the pupils are taught enough about germs and physiology so that they understand what contagion and dirt mean. The result is that the children themselves take every precaution to prevent sickness, and when a classmate is sick they see to it that quarantine is enforced and that the school doctor is notified.

The schools have carried on a pure milk campaign in the same way; the pupils brought samples of milk from home and tested it, and then saw that their parents did something about it if impurities were found. An anti-fly campaign goes on all the time and meets with a real response from the children. In the matter of health the schools not only do their share as a part of the whole community, they do more than this, acting as assistants to the board of health and getting rid of the prejudice and fear of city doctors which is so common in our foreign communities, and which makes it so hard to keep down disease and take care of school children. Once the coöperation and understanding of the children is gained by the city doctors, it is not hard to have their adenoids or eyes attended to. The children know why these things need to be done even if their parents do not, and they see to it that the parents are kept from interfering and that they help.

Another difficult problem for the public schools in an industrial community with a foreign population is to keep the children in school after the legal age at which they may leave. The Gary schools go about this just as they attack the question of public health, not by making more rules or trying compulsion, but by getting the children themselves to help, by making the schools so obviously useful for each individual that he wants to stay. There are no "High Schools" in Gary! A pupil goes to school in one building from the day he enters kindergarten until he is ready for college or until he goes into business or the factory. There is no graduation with a celebration and a diploma at the end of the eighth grade. When a pupil begins the ninth grade his program deviates from the plan of previous years, but otherwise there is nothing done to make the child think he has gone as far as he needs, that from now on he will simply be getting frills and luxuries. The teachers do not change. The same history, language and literature teachers conduct all the grades; and in the shops the pupils get a chance to learn some one thing thoroughly. The pupils do not look forward to the last four years of school with dread of a hard and useless grind, they look at it as a continuation of their school life, getting harder from year to year as their own ability increases. And especially they regard this period as an opportunity to get training whose immediate value they can see. The arguments of the school to persuade the pupils to stay in school are practical, telling arguments, things the children can see. The school press prints from time to time bulletins explaining to the pupils and their parents the opportunities that the Gary schools offer in the way of general education and of special training. These bulletins give statistics and information about the opportunities in the different fields of work; they show the boys and girls in figures the relative positions and salaries of high-school graduates and those who leave school at fourteen—as they appear one, two, or ten years after leaving school. Business men come to the schools and tell the students what the chances for graduates and non-graduates are in their business and why they want better educated employees. Statistics of Gary pupils are kept and shown to the pupils. The usual break between the eighth grade and high school does not exist, and, therefore, parents do not think it necessary to take their children out of school. They find that the sacrifices they have made to keep the children in can be kept up for a few years more. If children are going to learn a trade better by staying in school than by leaving, and if children are keen to continue in school with definite plans for the future, even the most poverty-stricken parent is unwilling to thwart the advantage of his children. It is well known that in big cities where the proportion of pupils who leave school at fourteen is overwhelming, and where the usual reason given is that the parents need the financial help of the children, the real reason for defection is the indifference of the pupils themselves to school. The almost invariable answer given by the child to the question, "Why did you leave school?" is, "Because I did not like it." This fact taken with the poverty at home is enough to make them leave school at the first chance. Give the child work that he recognizes as interesting and valuable and a chance to play, and his hatred of school will speedily be forgotten.

The inflexibility of the ordinary public school tends to push the pupils out of school instead of keeping them in. The curriculum does not fit them, and there is no way of making it fit without upsetting the entire organization of the school. One failure sets a pupil back in all his work, and he soon gets the feeling that his own efforts are not important, because the school machinery works on at the same rate, regardless of any individual pupil or study. Indifference or dislike is almost surely the result of feeling that work is making no impression, that the machine for which he is working is not after all affected or dependent upon his work. In Gary organization has been made to fit each individual child, and is flexible enough so that even the most difficult pupil can not upset its working. The child and the school get along together. We have explained in an earlier paragraph how the two-school system works so that an individual can spend more or less time on any one subject, or can drop it altogether. The child who is weak physically spends much of his time on the playground, while the child who is weak in arithmetic or geography can take these lessons with both schools or even with a grade below, and hundreds of children in the same building can make the same sort of change in their program without disturbing the orderly conduct of the school routine. A pupil who is stronger in one subject than in the rest of his work, can take that subject with a higher grade. The pupil who is losing interest in school and falling behind in most of his studies, or who is beginning to talk of leaving, is not punished for this lack of interest by being put still further back. His teachers find out in what he is good and give him plenty of time to work at it, and to get ahead in it so that his interest in his work is stimulated. If he later wakes up to an interest in the regular school program, so much the better. Every facility is given him to catch up with his grade in all the work. If this awakening does not come, the boy or girl has still been kept in school until he or she learned some one thing, probably the one most suited to the pupil's ability, instead of leaving or failing entirely by being held back in everything until even the one strong faculty died and the pupil was without either training or the moral stimulus of success.

The school program is reorganized every two months and the pupil may change his entire program at any one of these times, instead of having to struggle along for half a year with work that is too hard or too easy or not properly apportioned. For administrative convenience the schools still keep the grade classifications, but pupils are classified not according to the grade number, but as "rapid," "average," and "slow" workers. Rapid pupils finish the twelve years of school at about sixteen years of age, average workers at eighteen, and slow workers at twenty. This classification does not describe the quality of work done. The slow worker may be a more thorough scholar than the rapid

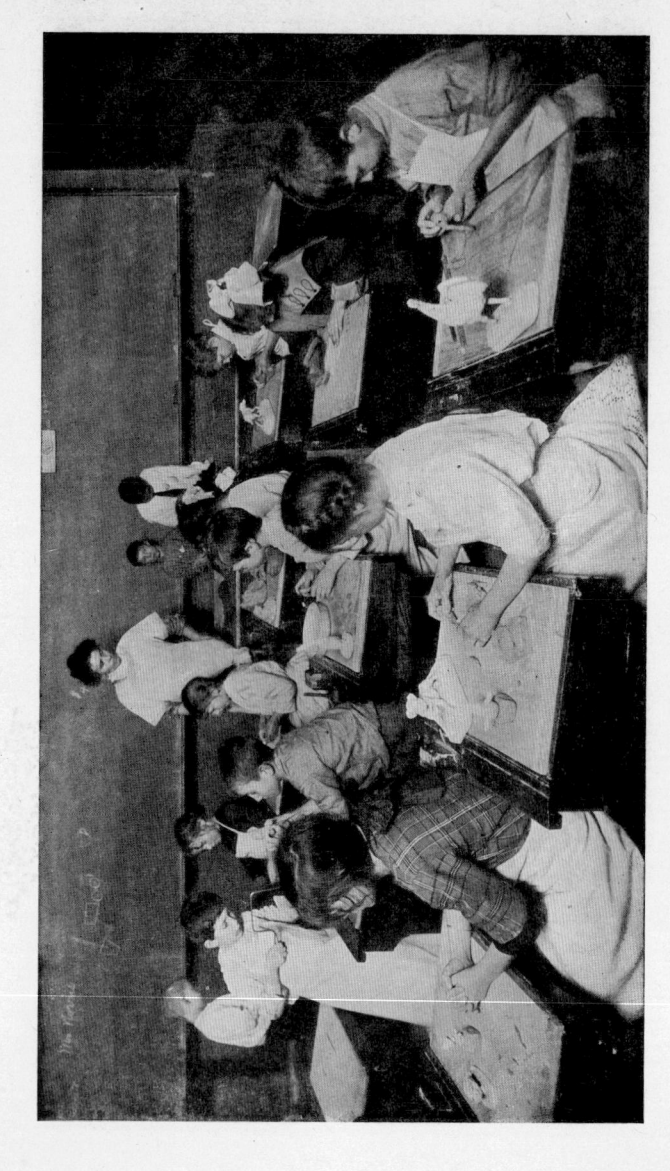

Special teachers for special subjects from the very beginning. (Gary, Ind.)

worker. The classification is used not to distinguish between the abilities of scholars, but to take advantage of the natural growth of the child by letting his work keep abreast with it. The rapid child moves as quickly as possible from grade to grade instead of being held back until his work has no stimulus for him, and the slow worker is not pushed into work before he is ready for it. Does this flexible system work successfully or does it result in easy-going, slap-dash methods? We have only to visit the schools and see the pupils hard at work, each one responsible for his own movements through the day, to be convinced that the children are happy and interested; while from the point of view of the teacher and educator, the answer is even more positively favorable, when we consult the school records. Fifty-seven per cent. of all the school children in Gary who are thirteen years old are in the seventh grade or above it. This is a better showing than most industrial communities can make, and means that the majority of all the Gary school children go through school at about the same rate as the average pupil who is preparing for college. Even more remarkable than this are the figures regarding the pupils who have gone on to higher schools or colleges after leaving the Gary schools. One-third of all the pupils that have left the Gary schools during the eight years of their existence are now in the state university, in an engineering school, or a business college. When we remember that the population of Gary is made up principally of laborers in the steel mills, and is sixty per cent. foreign born, and compare with this the usual school history of the second generation in this country, we realize how successful Mr. Wirt has been in making a system which meets the needs of the pupils, a system that appeals to the community as so good that they want to go on and get more education than mere necessity requires.

The motive back of these changes from the routine curriculum is always a social one. Mr. Wirt believes that if the social end of the school is properly emphasized the pedagogical will take care of itself. The public schools must study the needs and qualities of its pupils, the needs of the community and the opportunities that the community contributes to the schools' welfare. We have seen how the physical life of the child and the health of the community are used in the school curriculum, so as to make the curriculum more interesting, and for the good of the community as well. This same close connection is kept up between the school work and other community interests and matters of daily life. Every advantage is taken of the social instincts of children in the teaching. Instead of isolating each grade and cutting off the younger children from the older, the two are thrown together as much as possible. The younger grades use the laboratories and shops which would be an unwarranted extravagance if the high-school pupils were not in the same buildings and using them also for technical training. They use them not only for beginning lessons in science or manual training, but they go into them when the older classes are working there to act as helpers or as an audience for the higher grades. Fourth and fifth grade pupils thus assist seventh, eighth, and ninth grade students in shops, studios, and laboratories.

The older children learn responsibility and coöperation from having to look out for the little people, and the latter learn an astonishing amount about the subject from waiting on, watching, and asking questions of the older pupils. Both grades find out what is going on in the school and get thereby a large feeling of fellowship, while the interest of the lower one grows and finds reasons for staying in school. The work of the older children is used, wherever it is feasible, in teaching the lower grades. Maps and charts made in drawing are used for less advanced pupils in nature study or geography; the printing shop makes the spelling lists and problem sheets for the whole school; the doctor in his health campaigns calls in the art and English workers to make posters and pamphlets. The halls of the schools are hung with notices of what is going on in the school, with especially good and interesting drawings or maps, with information about what is being made in the different shops, or about anything that the whole school ought to see or know.

Another strong element in making public opinion is the auditorium, where every pupil in the school spends one hour each day, sometimes for choral singing, sometimes to hear an older grade tell about an interesting experiment in physics, to find out from a cooking class about cheap and nutritious bills of fare, or to hear the doctor tell how the school can improve the health conditions in its home neighborhoods. The auditorium period is for the use of the general community as well. Ministers, politicians, any one in the city who is doing anything interesting, may come in and tell the children about it. The school invites all social agencies in the neighborhood to come in in this way.

The hour for "application" contributes to the same end. The children go to the nearest public library to read or to look up references for their class work, or simply for a lesson on the use of library books; or they may go to the neighboring Y. M. C. A. building to use the gymnasium or to listen to a lecture; or they may go to any church or club that offers religious instruction desired by the parents. The school is a social clearing house for the neighborhood. The application period is also used to supplement the regular classroom studies by means of practical work in the shops or on the playground. Thus an arithmetic class may get a lesson in applied mathematics by laying out the foundation for a house on the playground, or by spending an hour in the school store, a room fitted up like a grocery store, where the children get practice in mental and oral arithmetic and in English by playing "store." The application period may also be spent in doing work for the school building. Thus an older pupil, studying stenography and typewriting or bookkeeping, might go to the school office and do an hour of real work, helping one of the clerks. The boys in the fifth grade put in this time in tending the school storeroom. They take entire charge of the school supplies, check up all the material sent in by the board and distributing it through the building to the teachers and janitors. The records of the pupils in the different shops are kept by other pupils in their application time. One paid bookkeeper has general charge of an office, where the pupils come with printed slips filled out by the shop teacher, giving them credit for so much time at a certain rate of skill; the pupil clerks give the pupils credit on their record for this work and keep all the records. Pupils also run a post office for the building, and the writer saw a sixth grade boy delivering salary checks and collecting receipts for them through the building. Children who do this kind of work are not only learning arithmetic and bookkeeping, they are learning as well responsibility and reliability. They get an appreciation of what their school means, and are made wide-awake to its welfare; they learn that they are the real school, identical with its interests.

The school lunch room is conducted by the cooking department. When the Emerson School was first built it was equipped with the regulation cooking school desks, individual gas burners, tables and lockers. All this has since been turned into a serving table where student waiters serve the food they have cooked—real lunches to their fellow students, who pay a student cashier. The younger girls get their cooking lessons by going to the older girls' cooking lessons as helpers and watchers. The girls do all the menu planning and buying for the lunch room and keep the accounts. They have to pay expenses and serve menus that come up to the standard set by the chemistry department, where they have analyzed food and made tables of comparative values. The result is steaming hot food, nourishing and well cooked, sold very cheaply. The daily menu is posted with the price of each article and its food value, and the walls of the lunch room are hung with posters and charts showing the relative values of foodstuffs, sample menus for cheap and nourishing meals, and the extravagance of poor food. These have all been made by the cooking school students and are the result of actual experimentation.

Gary schools do not teach civics out of a textbook. Pupils learn civics by helping to take care of their own school building, by making the rules for their own conduct in the halls and on the playgrounds, by going into the public library, and by listening to the stories of what Gary is doing as told by the people who are doing it. They learn by a mock campaign, with parties, primaries, booths and ballots for the election of their own student council. Pupils who have made the furniture and the cement walks with their own hands, and who know how much it cost, are slow to destroy walks or furniture, nor are they going to be very easily fooled as to the value they get in service and improvements when they themselves become taxpayers. The health campaigns, the application work which takes them to the social agencies of the city, the auditorium periods when they learn more about their city, all give civics lessons that make their own appeal. The children can see the things with their own eyes; they are learning citizenship by being good citizens.

The value of this practical civics is doubly great because of the large number of children with foreign parents, who know nothing about the government or organization of the city in which they are living, and who, because they do not understand what they see about them, cannot know its possibilities and limitations. The parents learn nothing of the laws until they break them, of public health until they endanger it, nor of social resources until they want something. They are naturally suspicious of government and social authority in consequence, and it is very important that their children should have some real knowledge on which to base a sounder judgment. Besides giving them this, the schools try to teach American standards of living to the pupils and so to their parents. On entering school every pupil gives the school office, besides the usual name, age, and address, certain information about his family, its size, its resources, and the character of the home he lives in. This record is kept in the school and transferred if the child moves out of the school district. Every grade teacher takes a certain number of squares in the school district, and they make plans of this area. The children make a large scale map, with streets, walks, lamp posts and mail boxes, locating every house, barn, or shed and every empty lot. This is altered as changes are made. Every child brings measurements of the rooms in his home and draws a floor plan of his house. These plans are kept with the teacher's map of her district, so that she has a complete map of the neighborhood and home of every child living in it. By comparing these with any family record, it is a simple matter to tell if the family are living under proper moral and hygienic conditions.

The teacher has a district small enough to know it thoroughly, and as far as possible she gets acquainted with all the children living in it. If bad conditions are due to ignorance or poverty, the teacher finds out what can be done to remedy them, and sees to it that the family learn how they can better themselves. If conditions are very bad, neighborhood public opinion is worked up through the other children on the block. From time to time an auditorium period is devoted to showing these maps and pointing out the good and bad features of blocks and neighborhoods. Children always carry the news home to their parents, and as rents and accommodations are freely discussed, these reports are often acted upon. The parents are encouraged to come to the school and ask for information, and on more than one occasion some newly arrived family has moved from an overcrowded rear shack to a comfortable flat with the same rent because through the children they found out that their bad quarters were unnecessary. Because the school does this work to help, and as part of its regular program, it is accepted by the children and their parents as a matter of course. Information about improvements, sanitation, the size and comfort of the houses, and the rents, is given to the parents. If a block is poor a good block near by where conditions are better and the rents the same, is shown them. Thus the schools not only teach the theory of good citizenship and social conditions, they give the children actual facts and conditions, so that they can see what is wrong and how it can be bettered.

Gary schools use the community as much as possible as a contributor to the educational facilities, and in so doing they give good return in immediate results, besides the larger return in alert and intelligent citizens. Conditions in Gary are not ideal. The schools have no larger sums to spend than any city of its size, the teachers might be found in any other town, and the pupils come for the most part from homes that offer their children no training, while the parents are trying to adjust themselves to entirely new surroundings. But these schools have done much by showing a good business management, by spending the taxpayers' money in an economical way so as to give the younger generation the largest possible facilities for spending their time profitably. The results of the system as seen in the school buildings and playgrounds, the alert and happy students, and the statistics of their progress through school as well as their careers afterwards, are doubly inspiring just because they have been accomplished with the resources available in any public school.

CHAPTER VIII

THE SCHOOL AS A SOCIAL SETTLEMENT

SCHOOLS all over the country are finding that the most direct way of vitalizing their work is through closer relations with local interests and occupations. That period of American school history which was devoted to building up uniformity of subject-matter, method, and administration, was obliged to neglect everything characteristic of the local environment, for attention to that meant deviation from uniformity. Things remote in time and space, and things of an abstract nature, are most readily reduced to uniformity and doled out in doses to children in a mass. Unfortunately the consequences were too often that in aiming to hit all children by exactly the same educational ammunition, none of them were really deeply touched. Efforts to bring the work into vital connection with pupils' experiences necessarily began to vary school materials to meet the special needs and definite features of local life.

This closer contact with immediate neighborhood conditions not only enriches school work and strengthens motive force in the pupils, but it increases the service rendered to the community. No school can make use of the activities of the neighborhood for purposes of instruction without this use influencing, in turn, the people of the neighborhood. Pupils, for example, who learn civics by making local surveys and working for local improvements, are certain to influence the life of the locality, while lessons in civics learned from the purely general statements of a text-book are much less likely to have either applicability or application. In turn, the community perceives the local efficiency of the schools. It realizes that the service rendered to welfare is not remote, to appear when the pupils become adults, but a part of the regular, daily course of education. The statement that the schools exist for a democratic purpose, for the good of citizenship, becomes an obvious fact and not a formula. A community which perceives what a strong factor its school is in civic activities, is quick to give support and assistance in return, either by extending the use of its own facilities (as happens in Gary) or by the direct assistance of labor, money, or material when these are needed.

The supervising principal of public school

No. 26 in Indianapolis is trying an experiment unlike any other known to us in an effort to make his plant a true school; that is, a place where the children of his neighborhood shall become healthy, happy, and competent both economically and socially, and where the connection of instruction with the life of the community shall be directly recognized both by children and parents. Mr. Valentine's school is located in the poor, crowded colored district of the city and has only colored pupils. It is not an attempt to solve the "race question" nor yet an experiment suited only to colored people. There is nothing in the school not entirely practical in any district where the children come from homes with limited resources and meager surroundings. A visitor when leaving this school can not fail to wish that such ventures might be started in all our great cities,—indeed in any community where people need to be aroused to a sense of their needs, including the fact that if they are to contribute to the best interests of the community, they must be taught how to earn a living, and how to use their resources for themselves and their neighbors both in leisure time and in working hours. Mr. Valentine's school is a school for colored children only in the sense that the work has been arranged in relation to the conditions in the neighborhood; these modify the needs of the particular children who are the pupils. Yet the success of the experiment would mean a real step forward in solving the "race question" and peculiar problems of any immigrant district as well. Mr. Valentine is not interested in illustrating any theories on these points, but in making up for gaps in the home life of the pupils; giving them opportunities to prepare for a better future; in supplying plenty of healthy occupation and recreation; and in seeing to it that their school work reacts at once to improve neighborhood conditions.

Mr. Valentine's school is really a social settlement for the neighborhood, but it has a decided advantage over the average settlement, for it comes in contact with all the children living within its district for a number of hours each day, while most settlements reach the children for only a few scattered hours each week. The school has a larger influence than most settlements because it is a public institution for which the people who use it are paying their share; they feel that their relation to it is a business one, not a matter of philanthropy. Because of this businesslike relation the school is able really to teach the doctrines of social welfare. In any settlement the work is always handicapped by the fact that the people who make use of it feel that they are receiving something for which they do not pay, that something is being done for them by people who are better off financially than they are. But giving a community facilities that it lacks for special classes and recreation through the public school of the district put the work on a different basis. The school is really the property of the people of the district; they feel that they are more or less responsible for what is done there. Any wider activities that a school may undertake are to a certain extent the work of the people themselves; they are simply making use of the school plant for their own needs.

The neighborhood around Mr. Valentine's school is one of the poorest in Indianapolis, and once had a bad reputation for lawlessness and disorder as well. The school had struggled along for years with little or no support from the community as a whole or from individual parents. The per cent. of truancy was high, and a large number of cases were sent to the juvenile court each year. The children took no interest in their work as a whole, and cases of extreme disorder were not infrequent; one pupil tried to revenge himself on his teacher for a merited punishment with a butcher's knife, in another case it was necessary to arrest a boy's father as a lesson to the neighborhood. Besides this attitude of hostility and of unwilling attendance, the school had to contend with immoral surroundings which finally made it necessary to do something to isolate the school building from neighboring houses. Finally the school board bought the tract of land and wooden tenements around the school building. It was at first proposed to tear down the old buildings, but the authorities were persuaded to turn them over to the school for its use. The school now found itself the possessor of a large playground and of three frame tenements in the worst possible condition, the board having stipulated that this added property should mean no further expense to the city after its purchase and the cleaning up of the grounds. It was decided to use the buildings for social and industrial purposes. One of them was fitted up by the pupils and neighbors interested as a manual training building. In this there is a carpenter shop, a sewing room, and a room for the class in shoemaking. Each grade devotes a regular number of hours a week to hand work, and has an opportunity to join other industrial classes after school. The immediate practical appeal of the work is never lost sight of, and the work is arranged to fit the needs of the individual pupil.

The carpenter shop is open all day, and there are classes for the girls as well as for the boys. Pupils are at liberty to go into the shop and work whenever they have any free time. The work is not confined to exercises to train the child in the use of tools, but each pupil makes something that he needs or wants, something that will be of real use to him. Processes and control of tools are taught the pupil by means of the piece of work he is doing. This is the keynote to all the industrial work done in the school. The more remote end of teaching the child processes which will be useful to him later is not lost sight of, but material is always used which has some immediate value to the child or to the school. The boys have learned carpentry work by making things that were needed in the school building—tables, cupboards, and bookcases—and by doing some of the repairing on the building. The girls have learned to sew by making clothes for themselves, for their brothers and sisters, and by making curtains and linen for the school. They have learned to cook by making soup for hot lunches for the school and the neighbors, and by cooking a whole meal for their own class. Besides the cooking and sewing department for the girls, there is a class in millinery and in crocheting. These two classes are conducted from the commercial point of view, to teach the girls to do something that will enable them to earn some money. In the millinery class the pupils start by making and trimming hats for themselves, so that they learn the different processes in the trade. The girls in the class who show the most skill are then allowed to take orders from friends and neighbors and trim or make hats for them. Besides the cost of the material the buyer pays a very small sum for the work, and this goes into the school treasury. The millinery class has done quite a business in the neighborhood, and turned out some very successful hats. Crocheting is taught as a trade, and any girl who wishes to make some money has an opportunity to learn how to make lace, table doilies, and all sorts of crocheted articles, like hoods, etc., which will sell. As the girls are learning, they are working on something which they can use for themselves or in their homes.

The work for the boys is arranged in the same way. Besides the carpenter work and the repairing there is a boys' cooking class, a shoe-repairing department, and a tailoring shop. The cooking class is even more popular with the boys than with the girls. In the shoe-repairing shop, which holds classes after school hours, the boys learn to mend their own shoes. A professional cobbler is the teacher, and the mending must be neatly done. The boys begin work on their own old shoes and as they progress in skill, are allowed to bring shoes from home to be repaired, or to mend for the girls and for the younger boys in the school, who, however, pay a small sum for the work. The tailoring department is run on the same plan, to teach habits of personal neatness and of industry through giving the pupils work that results in neatness and gives some manual skill and control of tools. The class is taught by a tailor, and the boys learn to patch and mend their own clothes, as well as to sponge and press them. Attendance is entirely voluntary, and the class meets after the regular school work is over. Knowing how to keep themselves tidy has resulted in a very marked improvement in the appearance and habits of the boys in the class, and has had an influence not only on the whole school, but on the neighborhood as well. The boys no longer resent the attempts of the teachers to influence them towards cleanliness and neatness, for they have become conscious of the advantages of these habits.

The cooking and domestic science classes are taught in one of the tenements turned over to the school without having been repaired, although the cooking equipment was supplied by the city. All the other work on the building—cleaning, painting, repairing, furnishing, and decorating —was done and paid for by the pupils of the school with help from the neighborhood clubs that use the building. There is a large cooking room, a demonstration dining and sitting room, and two bedrooms. The girls not only learn to cook real meals, but they learn how to serve them, and then how to take care of the demonstration house. The domestic science classes include lessons in buying, the comparative costs and values of food, something of food chemistry and values, and large quantity cooking. This work is done in connection with the soup kitchen. A group of girls have charge of the kitchen long enough to really learn about the work. They plan the menu and do the buying, cooking and serving of the soup, selling it for three cents a bowl to the pupils of the school and to neighbors. They keep all the accounts and not only have to make all their expenses,

THE SCHOOL AS A SETTLEMENT

but are expected to make some profit for the use of the school as well. They have made enough profit in one year to furnish most of the demonstration house. Aside from teaching how to do housework thoroughly and easily, the purpose of the house is to furnish an example of what can be done to make one of the regular frame tenements of the district comfortable and attractive, without more expense than most of the people now put into their homes. The house is very simply furnished, with cheap and strong things, in plain colors that are easily kept clean; the painting and papering was done by the pupils. The sewing class has made all the curtains and linen for the house, and made furniture by covering boxes, etc. Besides the class work that goes on in the building, the rooms are also used as a social center for the girls of the school.

The third building left standing on the ground purchased by the school authorities has been turned into a boys' club house. There is a gymnasium, two club rooms, and a shower bath room. This house was in exceedingly bad condition when it became part of the school property, and there was no money and not much lumber available to repair it. But the boys of the school wanted the club house, and were not discouraged because it was not given to them all finished. They started out, as they had done in the manual training and domestic science buildings, to do the work themselves. Under the direction of the manual training teacher, they pulled off old paper and broken plaster, tore up uneven floors and took out partitions. Then they laid floors, put in woodwork and painted it, rehung doors, mended windows, and made furniture and gymnastic apparatus. When there was a job they could not do, such as the plastering and plumbing, they went among their friends and asked for money or help in work. Plumbers and plasterers who lived near the school came in and gave their time and work to help the boys get their building in order, and other friends gave enough money to finish the work. Men in the neighborhood dug a long ditch through the school grounds for sewerage connections. Gradually they are adding to the gymnasium apparatus and to the simple bathing facilities, while cleaning and keeping up the painting continue to supply opportunities for useful work.

As already indicated, the reflex effect upon homes in the vicinity has been marked. The school board had intended to wreck the three tenement houses when they bought the land; but Mr. Valentine saw the opportunity to give the community something which they needed, and at the same time to arouse a spirit of cooperation and interest among both parents and pupils in place of the old spirit of distrust and antagonism, when he persuaded the board to turn the buildings over to the school. He told the pupils what could be done with them and asked for their help in doing it. He got a hearty response at once, and so went out into the district with the children and told their parents what he proposed to do and asked for help. He got the same generous response for the first building, the manual training shops, as for the boys' club. Besides the time and material which the skilled workers of the community have contributed, the community has given $350 in cash, no small sum for people as poor as they are. The value of the work being done in these buildings and of the training the boys have had in making them over, is proved by the fact that the community and the boys themselves wanted the work badly enough to pay for getting it in money and work. While it has undoubtedly been a struggle for the school and the district to contribute so much, the benefit to the school and to the community has been greater just because of these sacrifices and struggles. The work has made over the relations between the school and the pupils. The children like to go to school now, where before they had to be forced to go with threats of the truant officer, and their behavior is better when they get to school. The children's parents have changed their attitude in the same way. They not only see that the children go to school, but they want them to go because they appreciate that the school is giving them things they need to make them self-supporting; but they also see that they have their own share to do if the work is to be successful. The school has been the cause of the growth of community spirit in increased civic and social activities of the district. With improved attendance and discipline, the number of cases sent to the juvenile court has decreased one-half in proportion to the number of pupils in school. Meanwhile the educational value of the work done has undoubtedly been greater than that of work done in disconnected shops and kitchens.

The school is also carrying on definite work to arouse the pupils to a sense of responsibility for their community and neighbors. Giving the pupils as much liberty and respon-

(1) The boys like cooking more than the girls do.
(2) Mending their own shoes, to learn cobbling.
   (Public School 26, Indianapolis.)

sibility as possible around the school buildings is an important factor. Each pupil in the higher grades is given some small child in one of the lower grades to look out for On the playground they see to it that the charge has a fair chance to play, and that he behaves himself; they see that the little boy or girl comes to school clean and tidy, if necessary doing the washing or mending themselves. This work has proved especially successful in doing away with bullying and in arousing personal pride and a sense of responsibility in the older children; the younger ones are better looked after than before and have many opportunities to learn things from the older and more advanced pupils. The older pupils are also encouraged in every way to help in carrying on the outside activities of the school. They make calls and write notes to keep up the attendance at the night school; they see to the order of the principal's office and keep the boys' club house in order. All the teachers of the school are agreed upon a policy of frank discussion of the poverty of the district, and of urging the pupils to earn money to help their parents by becoming as nearly self-supporting as possible. Each grade keeps track of what its members earn and how they earn it, and the grade with the largest sum to its credit feels that it has accomplished something worth while during the year.

There is a savings bank in the school to teach the children habits of thrift and economy; here a pupil may deposit any sum from a penny up. The pupil receives a bank book in which stamps are pasted for his deposits, the money being kept in a city savings bank. The school also has a branch library, and the pupils are taught how to use it. Part of the playground has been made into a school garden, and here every pupil in the higher grades has a garden plot, also instruction which enables him to grow successfully some of the commoner fruits and flowers. This work is made very practical; the children have the sort of garden that would be useful and ornamental if it were in their own back yard. The school carries on a neighborhood campaign for home gardens, and the pupils with school gardens do much of this work, telling the people who want gardens what to plant, and giving them practical help with their plot until it is well established. In all these ways the teachers are trying to make ambitious, responsible citizens out of the student body. Inside the school pupils are taught higher standards of living than prevail in their homes, and they are taught as well trades and processes which will at least give them a start towards prosperity, and then, too, they are aroused to a feeling of responsibility for the welfare of the whole community.

All these things are done as part of the regular work of the school, and to a large extent during regular school hours. But there are many other activities which, while not contributing so directly to the education of the children, are important for the general welfare of the whole community. There is a night school for the adults of the neighborhood who want to go on learning, the shops being used as well as the schoolrooms. A group of people especially interested in the school have formed a club to promote the interest of the night school, and to see that the men of the community understand the opportunities it offers for them to perfect themselves in a trade or in their knowledge and use of English. This club is made up of men who live near the school and who are sufficiently alive to the needs of the school and the community to work very hard to let all the district know what the school is already doing for its welfare and what it can do as the people come to demand more and more from it. Besides keeping up the attendance at the night school, the club has done much for the general welfare of the school, like helping raise money for remodeling the buildings and giving an expensive phonograph to the school. The success of the school as a social center and the need for such a center are realized when we remember that this club is made up of men who live in the district, whose children are using the school, and who are perhaps themselves going to the night school.

There is also a vacation school during the summer time for the children of the neighborhood, with some classroom work and a great deal of time spent on the playground and in the workshops. The school has an active alumni association which uses the school building for social purposes and keeps track of the pupils that leave. A parents' club has been started as an aid in gaining the coöperation of the pupils' parents in the work of the school and as a means of finding out the real needs of the neighborhood. The parents are brought in even closer contact with the school through the series of teas given by the grades for their parents during the year. Each grade serves tea once a year in the domestic science house for the mothers of its pupils. The children do the work for the teas as part of their domestic science work, and write the invitations in their English class. The teachers use these teas as an opportunity for visiting the children's homes and getting acquainted with their mothers. The teacher who knows the home conditions of each child is much better able to adjust the work to the child, being aware of his weak and strong points. To poverty-stricken, overworked mothers these social gatherings come as a real event.

The pupils of the school are given social as well as educational opportunities through their school life. The boys' club house is opened nearly every night to local boys' clubs, some of them being school organizations and some independent ones. There are rooms for the boys to hold meetings and to play games, and a well-equipped gymnasium. The teachers of the school take turns supervising these evening gatherings. The attendance is large for the size of the building. Giving the boys a place for wholesome activities has done much to break up the habits of street loafing and the gangs which were so common in the district. The girls of the school use the domestic science house for social purposes. Two chapters of the Camp Fire girls hold regular meetings in the building and get help and advice from the teachers. Each domestic science class aims to teach the girls how to live a comfortable and self-respecting life, as well as how to do housework, and so becomes a social center of its own. The girls learn to cook and serve good cheap meals, and then they sit down together and eat what they have cooked. They talk over their individual problems with the teacher and with each other, and give each other much practical help. The domestic science teacher helps the girls who have some skill find work to do after school hours so that they can help their families by helping themselves; she helps the pupils find steady work as they leave school and then keeps track of them, encouraging them to go on fitting themselves for better work.

The success of the settlement work the school has done points strongly to the fact that the schoolhouse is the natural and logical social center in a neighborhood, the teachers coming into closer and more natural contact with both children and parents than is possible in the case of other district workers.

There are large economies combining the school and the settlement in districts where the social and economic standards of living are so low that the people are not especially successful citizens. Both the school and settlement facilities are enlarged by using the same group of buildings for both purposes. The settlement has the use of better and larger shops and classrooms than most settlements can command, and the school uses the social rooms and activities to become itself a community. The school comes in contact with almost all the families in a district so that community action is much easier to establish. But even more important than these economies are the far-reaching results which come from the fact that the school settlement is a democratic community, really reflecting the conditions of the community.

In using the school plant for any activities, whether simply for the usual eight classes or to supply the community with all sorts of opportunities, as the Gary schools are doing and as Mr. Valentine's school is doing, the people of the community feel that they are using for their own ends public facilities which have been paid for by their taxes. They want to see real, tangible results in the way of more prosperous and efficient families and better civic conditions, coming from the increased plant in the district school. Because the schools are public institutions in fact as well as in name, people know whether the schools are really meeting their needs and they are willing to work to see that they do. The school settlement reaps all the advantages of working for definite ends and of having the businesslike coöperation of the community as a body. In spite of the fact that the work of Mr. Valentine's school has been hampered by lack of funds, and that some of the special things done are suited to one particular local population, the changes which have taken place in the neighborhood in the relation between the school and the parents, and in the spirit of the pupils in their school attitude, show what a public school may mean to its neighborhood when it ceases to be an isolated academic institution.

The Gary schools and Mr. Valentine's school have effected an entire reorganization in order to meet the particular needs of the children of the community, physically, intellectually, and socially. Both schools are looking towards a larger social ideal; towards a community where the citizens will be prosperous and independent, where there will be no poverty-ridden population unable to produce good citizens. While changes in social conditions must take place before this can happen, these schools believe that such an education as they provide is one of the natural ways and perhaps the surest way of helping along the changes. Teaching people from the time they are children to think clearly and to take care of themselves is one of the best safeguards against exploitation.

A great many schools are doing some of the same sort of work, using the activities of the community as a means of enriching the curriculum, and using the school plant for a neighborhood center. The civic clubs of the Chicago public schools, which have already been described, are aiming at the same thing: the better equipment of pupils for their life in the community with the hope of improving the community itself. The Cottage School at Riverside, Illinois, where pupils all come from well-to-do American families, has found a similar club valuable for the pupils and of real use to the town. The school organized by the pupils into a civic league has made itself responsible for the conditions of the streets in certain portions of the town, and is not only cleaning up but trying to get the rest of the town interested in the problem. Mock elections and "self-governments" based upon political organization are examples of attempts of education to meet the need for training in good citizenship. Using the school plant as a social center is recognition of the need for social change and of the community's responsibility to help effect it.

The attempt to make this enlarged use of the school plant is not so much in order to train young people so that they can assume the burden of improvement for themselves as to give the neighborhood some immediate opportunities which it lacks for recreation, intercourse and improvement. The school plant is the natural and convenient place for such undertakings. Every community has the right to expect and demand that schools supported at public expense for public ends shall serve community uses as widely as possible. As attempts in socializing education have met with such success and such enthusiasm among the children that their value as educational tools is established, so giving the people of the community a real share in activities centered in school buildings and employing school equipment, is one of the surest ways of giving them a more intelligent public spirit and a greater interest in the right education of the youth of the land.

CHAPTER IX

INDUSTRY AND EDUCATIONAL READJUSTMENT

THE chief effort of all educational reforms is to bring about a readjustment of existing scholastic institutions and methods so that they shall respond to changes in general social and intellectual conditions. The school, like other human institutions, acquires inertia and tends to go on doing things that have once got started, irrespective of present demands. There are many topics and methods in existing education which date back to social conditions which are passing away. They are perpetuated because of tradition and custom. Especially is it true of our institutions of learning that their controlling ideals and ideas were fixed when industrial methods differed radically from those of the present. They grew up when the place of industry in life was much less important than it is now when practically all political and social affairs are bound up with economic questions. They were formed when there was no positive connection between science and the operations of production and distribution of goods; while at the present, manufacturing, railways, electric transportation, and all the agencies of daily life, represent just so much applied science. Economic changes have brought about a closer interdependence among men and strengthened the ideal of mutual service. These political, intellectual, and moral changes make questions connected with industrial education the most important problem of present-day public education in America.

The fact that the Greek word from which our word "school" is derived meant *leisure* suggests the nature of the change which has taken place. It is true at *all* times that education means relief from the pressure of having to make a living. The young have to be supported more or less by others while they are being instructed. They must be saved from the impact of the struggle for material existence. Opposition to child labor goes hand in hand with the effort to extend the facilities of public schools to all the wards of the nation. There must be free time for schooling, and pupils must not come to their studies physically worn out. Moreover, the use of imagination, thought and emotion in education demands minds which are free from harassing questions of self-support.

There must be an atmosphere of leisure if there is to be a truly liberal or free education.

Such things are as true now as when schools were named after the idea of leisure. But there was once assumed a permanent division between a leisure class and a laboring class. Education, beyond at least the mere rudiments, was intended only for the former. Its subject-matter and its methods were designed for those who were sufficiently well off so that they did not have to work for a living. The stigma attached to working with the hands was especially strong. In aristocratic and feudal countries such work was done by slaves or serfs, and the sense of social inferiority attached to these classes naturally led to contempt for the pursuits in which they were engaged. Training for them was a servile sort of education, while *liberal* education was an education for a free man, and a free man was a member of the upper classes, one who did not have to engage in labor for his own support or that of others. The antagonism to industry which was generated extended itself to all activities requiring use of the hands. A "gentleman" would not use his hands or train them to skill, save for sport or war. To employ the hands was to do useful work for others, while to render personal service to others was a badge of a dependent social and political status.

Strange as it may seem, the very notions of knowledge and of mind were influenced by this aristocratic order of society. The less the body in general, and the hands and the senses in particular, were employed, the higher the grade of intellectual activity. True thought resulting in true knowledge was to be carried on wholly within the mind without the body taking any part at all. Hence studies which could be carried on with a minimum of physical action were alone the studies belonging to a liberal education. First in order came such things as philosophy, theology, mathematics, logic, etc., which were purely mental. Next in rank came literature and language, with grammar, rhetoric, etc. The pursuit of even what we call the fine arts was relegated to a lower grade, because success in painting, sculpture, architecture, etc., required technical and manual training. Music alone was exempt from condemnation, partly because vocal music did not require the training of the hands, and partly because music was used for devotional purposes. Otherwise education should train men to appreciate art, not to produce it.

These ideas and ideals persisted in educational theory and practice long after the political and industrial conditions which generated them had begun to give way. Practically all the conceptions associated with culture and cultural education were created when the immense superiority of a leisure class over all working classes was a matter of course. Refinement, polish, esthetic taste, knowledge of classic literatures, acquaintance with foreign languages and with branches of sciences which could be studied by purely "mental" means, and which were not put to practical uses, were the marks of culture, just as they were the marks of leisure time and superior wealth. The learned professions—divinity, law, and, to a less extent, medicine—were admitted upon suffrance to the sphere of higher education, for the manual element in the service rendered to others was not so great as in industrial pursuits. But professional education was looked upon with disparagement in contrast with a liberal education just because its aim was rendering service to others. And for a long time medicine in particular occupied a mediocre and dubious position just because it required personal attention to the bodily needs of others.

Opposition to the introduction into higher education of the natural sciences was due not only to the conservative dread of change on the part of established institutions, but also to the fact that these sciences emphasized the use of the senses (which are physical organs), of physical apparatus, and of manual skill required in its manipulation. Even the representatives of mathematical science joined those of literary studies in assuming that the natural sciences must be less cultural than sciences like geometry, algebra, and calculus, which could be pursued in a more purely mental way. Even when the progress of social changes forced more and more useful studies into the curriculum, the idea of a graded rank in the cultural value of studies persisted. Occupations like banking and commerce involved less manual activity and less direct personal service to others than housekeeping, manufacturing, and farming, consequently the studies which prepared for them were at least more "genteel" than studies having to do with the latter. Even at the present time many people associate mental activity with physical acquiescence.

The first breach in this order of ideas occurred in elementary education. Along with the spread of democratic ideas which took place in the eighteenth century, there developed the idea that education was a need and right of the masses as well as a privilege of the upper classes. In reading Rousseau and Pestalozzi, an American student, who is used to the democratic idea of universal education, is not likely to notice that their conception of the educational development of all as a social necessity is even more revolutionary than the particular methods which they urged. But such was the case. Even so enlightened a liberal as John Locke wrote his educational essay with reference to the education of a gentleman, and assumed that the training of the laboring classes should be of a radically different kind. The idea that all the powers of all members of society are capable of development and that society owed it to itself and to its constituent members to see that the latter received this development, was the first great intellectual token of the democratic revolution which was occurring. It is noteworthy that Rousseau was Swiss by birth, that democratic political ideas were rife in France when he wrote, and that Pestalozzi was not only Swiss by birth but did his work in that republican country.

While the development of public elementary schools for the masses inevitably puts emphasis upon the usefulness of studies as a reason for education, the growth of the public curriculum and methods was profoundly affected by the surviving ideals of leisure class education. Elementary education, just because it was an education for the masses, was regarded as a kind of necessary political and economic concession rather than as a serious educative enterprise. A strict line was drawn between it, with its useful studies, and the higher education of the few conducted for genuinely cultural purposes. Reading, writing, arithmetic, the three R's, were to be taught because of their utility. They were needed to make individuals capable of self-support, of "getting on" better, and so capable of rendering better economic service under changed commercial conditions. It was assumed that the greater number of pupils would leave school as soon as they had mastered the practical use of these tools.

No better evidence could be found that primary education is still regarded with respect to the larger number of pupils, as a practical social necessity, not as an intrinsic educative measure, than the fact that the greater number of pupils leave school about the fifth grade —that is, when they have acquired rudimentary skill in reading, writing and figuring. The opposition of influential members of the community to the introduction of any studies, save perhaps geography and history, beyond the three R's, the tendency to regard other things as "frills and fads," is evidence of the way in which purely elementary schooling is regarded. A fuller and wider culture in literature, science and the arts may be allowed in the case of those better off, but the masses are not to be educatively developed so much as trained in the use of tools needed to make them effective workers. Elementary instruction to a larger extent than we usually admit, is a substitute, under the changed circumstances of production and distribution of goods, for the older apprenticeship system. The latter was never treated as educational in a fundamental sense; the former is only partially conducted as a thoroughly educational enterprise.

In part the older ideals of a predominantly literary and "intellectual" education invaded and captured the new elementary schools. For the smaller number of pupils who might go on to a higher and cultural education, the three R's were the tools of learning, the only really indispensable tools of acquiring knowledge. They are all of them concerned with language, that is, with *symbols* of facts and ideas, a fact which throws a flood of light upon the prevailing ideas of learning and knowledge.

Knowledge consists of the ready-made material which others have found out, and mastery of language is the means of access to this fund. To learn is to appropriate something from this ready-made store, not to find out something for one's self. Educational reformers may go on attacking pouring-in methods of teaching and passive reception methods of learning; but as long as these ideas of the nature of knowledge are current, they make little headway. The separation of the activity of the mind from the activity of the senses in direct observation and from the activity of the hand in construction and manipulation, makes the material of studies academic and remote, and compels the passive acquisition of information imparted by textbook and teacher.

In the United States there was for a long time a natural division of labor between the book-learning of the schools and the more direct and vital learning of out-of-school life. It is impossible to exaggerate the amount of mental and moral training secured by our forefathers in the course of the ordinary pursuits of life. They were engaged in subduing a new country. Industry was at a premium, and instead of being of a routine nature, pioneer conditions required initiative, ingenuity, and pluck. For the most part men were working for themselves; or, if for others, with a prospect of soon becoming masters of their own affairs. While the citizens of old-world monarchies had no responsibility for the conduct of government, our forefathers were engaged in the experiment of conducting their own government. They had the incentive of a participation in the conduct of civic and public affairs which came directly home to them. Production had not yet been concentrated in factories in congested centers, but was distributed through villages. Markets were local rather than remote. Manufacturing was still literally *hand-making,* with the use of local water-power; it was not carried on by big machines to which the employed "hands" were mechanical adjuncts. The occupations of daily life engaged the imagination and enforced knowledge of natural materials and processes.

Children as they grew up either engaged in or were in intimate contact with spinning, weaving, bleaching, dyeing, and the making of clothes; with lumbering, and leather, saw-mills, and carpentry; with working of metals and making of candles. They not only saw the grain planted and reaped, but were familiar with the village grist-mill and the preparation of flour and of foodstuffs for cattle. These things were close to them, the processes were all open to inspection. They knew where things came from and how they were made or where they went to, and they knew these things by personal observation. They had the discipline that came from sharing in useful activities.

While there was too much taxing toil, there was also stimulus to imagination and training of independent judgment along with the personal knowledge of materials and processes. Under such conditions, the schools could hardly have done better than devote themselves to books, and to teaching a command of the use of books, especially since, in most communities, books, while a rarity and a luxury, were the sole means of access to the great world beyond the village surroundings.

But conditions changed and school materials and methods did not change to keep pace. Population shifted to urban centers. Production became a mass affair, carried on in big factories, instead of a household affair. Growth of steam and electric transportation brought about production for distant markets, even for a world market. Industry was no longer a local or neighborhood concern. Manufacturing was split up into a very great variety of separate processes through the economies incident upon extreme division of labor. Even the workingmen in a particular line of industry rarely have any chance to become acquainted with the entire course of production, while outsiders see practically nothing but either the raw material on one hand or the finished product on the other. Machines depend in their action upon complicated facts and principles of nature which are not recognized by the worker unless he has had special intellectual training. The machine worker, unlike the older hand worker, is following blindly the intelligence of others instead of his own knowledge of materials, tools, and processes. With the passing of pioneer conditions passed also the days when almost every individual looked forward to being at some time in control of a business of his own. Great masses of men have no other expectation than to be permanently hired for pay to work for others. Inequalities of wealth have multiplied, so that demand for the labor of children has become a pressing menace to the serious education of great numbers. On the other hand, children in wealthy families have lost the moral and practical discipline that once came from sharing in the round of home duties. For a large number there is little alternative, especially in larger cities, between irksome child labor and demoralizing child idleness. Inquiries conducted by competent authorities show that in the great centers of population opportunities for play are so inadequate that free time is not even spent in wholesome recreations by a majority of children.

These statements do not begin, of course, to cover the contrasts between present social conditions and those to which our earlier school facilities were adapted. They suggest, however, some of the obvious changes with which education must reckon if it is to maintain a vital connection with contemporary social life, so as to give the kind of instruction needed to make efficient and self-respecting members of the community. The sketch would be even more incomplete, however, if it failed to note that along with these changes there has been an immense cheapening of printed material and an immense increase in the facilities for its distribution. Libraries abound, books are many and cheap, magazines and newspapers are everywhere. Consequently the schools do not any longer bear the peculiar relation to books and book knowledge which they once did. While out of school conditions have lost many of the educative features they once possessed, they have gained immensely in the provision they make for reading matter and for stimulating interest in reading. It is no longer necessary or desirable that the schools should devote themselves so exclusively to this phase of instruction. But it is more necessary than it used to be that the schools shall develop such interest in the pupils as will induce them to read material that is intellectually worth while.

While merely learning the use of language symbols and of acquiring habits of reading is less important than it used to be, the question of the use to which the power and habits shall be put is much more important. To learn to use reading matter means that schools shall arouse in pupils problems and interests that lead students both in school and after they leave school to seek that subject-matter of history, science, biography, and literature which is inherently valuable, and not to waste themselves upon the trash which is so abundantly provided. It is absolutely impossible to secure this result when schools devote themselves to the formal sides of language instead of to developing deep and vital interest in subject-matter. Educational theorists and school authorities who attempt to remedy the deplorable reading habits with which many youth leave school by means of a greater amount of direct attention to language studies and literatures, are engaged in a futile task. Enlargement of intellectual horizon, and awakening to the multitude of interesting problems presented by contemporary conditions, are the surest guarantees for good use of time with books and magazines. When books are made an end in themselves, only a small and highly specialized class will devote themselves to really serviceable books. When there is a lively sense of the interest of social affairs, all who possess the sense will turn as naturally to the books which foster that interest as to the other things of which they feel a need.

These are some of the reasons for saying that the general problem of readjustment of education to meet present conditions is most acute at the angle of industry. The various details may be summed up in three general moral principles. First, never before was it as important as it is now that each individual should be capable of self-respecting, self-supporting, *intelligent* work—that each should make a living for himself and those dependent upon his efforts, and should make it with an intelligent recognition of what he is doing and an intelligent interest in doing his work well. Secondly, never before did the work of one individual affect the welfare of others on such a wide scale as at present.

Modern conditions of production and exchange of commodities have made the whole world one to a degree never approximated before. A war to-day may close banks and paralyze trade in places thousands of miles away from the scene of action. This is only a coarse and sensational manifestation of an interdependence which is quietly and persistently operating in the activity of every farmer, manufacturer, laborer, and merchant, in every part of the civilized globe. Consequently there is a demand which never existed before that all the items of school instruction shall be seen and appreciated in their bearing upon the network of social activities which bind people together. When men lived in small groups which had little to do with each other, the harm done by an education which pursued exclusively intellectual and theoretic aims was comparatively slight. Knowledge might be isolated because men were isolated. But to-day the accumulation of information, just as information, apart from its social bearings, is worse than futile. Acquisition of modes of skill apart from realization of the social uses to which they may be put is fairly criminal. In the third place, industrial methods and processes depend to-day upon knowledge of facts and laws of natural and social science in a much greater degree than ever before. Our railways and steamboats, traction cars, telegraphs, and telephones, factories and farms, even our ordinary household appliances, depend for their existence upon intricate mathematical, physical, chemical, and biological insight. They depend for their best ultimate use upon an understanding of the facts and relationships of social life. Unless the mass of workers are to be blind cogs and pinions in the apparatus they employ, they must have some understanding of the physical and social facts behind and ahead of the material and appliances with which they are dealing.

Thus put, the problem may seem to be so vast and complicated as to be impossible of solution. But we must remember that we are dealing with a problem of readjustment, not of original creation. It will take a long time to complete the readjustment which will be brought about gradually. The main thing now is to get started, and to start in the right direction. Hence the great importance of the various experimental steps which have already been taken. And we must also remember that the essential thing to be brought about through the change is not amassing more information, but the formation of certain attitudes and interests, ways of looking at things and dealing with them. If accomplishment of the educational readjustment meant that pupils must become aware of the whole scope of scientific and social material involved in the occupations of daily life, the problem would be absolutely impossible of solution. But in reality accomplishing the reform means *less* attention than under present conditions to mere bulk of knowledge.

What is wanted is that pupils shall form the habit of connecting the limited information they acquire with the activities of life, and gain ability to connect a limited sphere of human activity with the scientific principles upon which its successful conduct depends. The attitudes and interests thus formed will then take care of themselves. If we take arithmetic or geography themselves as subjects isolated from social activities and uses, then the aim of instruction must be to cover the whole ground. Any failure to do so will mark a defect in learning. But not so if what we, as educators, are concerned with is that pupils shall realize the connection of what they learn about number, or about the earth's surface, with vital social activities. The question ceases to be a matter simply of quantity and becomes one of motive and purpose. The problem is not the impossible one of acquainting the pupil with all the social uses to which knowledge of number is put, but of teaching him in such a way that each step which he takes in advance in his knowledge of number shall be connected with some situation of human need and activity, so that he shall see the bearing and application of what is learnt. Any child who enters upon the study of number already has experiences which involve number. Let his instruction in arithmetic link itself to these everyday social activities in which he already shares, and, as far as it goes, the problem of socializing instruction is solved.

The industrial phase of the situation comes in, of course, in the fact that these social experiences have their industrial aspect. This does not mean that his number work shall be crassly utilitarian, or that all the problems shall be in terms of money and pecuniary gain or loss. On the contrary, it means that the pecuniary side shall be relegated to its proportionate place, and emphasis put upon the place occupied by knowledge of weight, form, size, measure, numerical quantity, as well as money, in the carrying on of the activities of life. The purpose of the readjustment of education to existing social conditions is not to substitute the acquiring of money or of bread and butter for the acquiring of information as an educational aim. It is to supply men and women who as they go forth from school shall be intelligent in the pursuit of the activities in which they engage. That a part of that intelligence will, however, have to do with the place which bread and butter actually occupy in the lives of people to-day, is a necessity. Those who fail to recognize this fact are still imbued, consciously or unconsciously, with the intellectual prejudices of an aristocratic state. But the primary and fundamental problem is not to prepare individuals to work at particular callings, but to be vitally and sincerely interested in the calling upon which they must enter if they are not to be social parasites, and to be informed as to the social and scientific bearings of that calling. The aim is not to prepare bread-winners. But since men and women are normally engaged in bread-winning vocations, they need to be intelligent in the conduct of households, the care of children, the management of farms and shops, and in the political conduct of a democracy where industry is the prime factor.

The problem of educational readjustment thus has to steer between the extremes of an inherited bookish education and a narrow, so-called practical, education. It is comparatively easy to clamor for a retention of traditional materials and methods on the ground that they alone are liberal and cultural. It is comparatively easy to urge the addition of narrow vocational training for those who, so it is assumed, are to be the drawers of water and the hewers of wood in the existing economic régime, leaving intact the present bookish type of education for those fortunate enough not to have to engage in manual labor in the home, shop, or farm. But since the real question is one of reorganization of all education to meet the changed conditions of life—scientific, social, political—accompanying the revolution in industry, the experiments which have been made with this wider end in view are especially deserving of sympathetic recognition and intelligent examination.

CHAPTER X

EDUCATION THROUGH INDUSTRY

THE experiments of some of our cities in giving their children training which shall make them intelligent in all the activities of their life, including the important one of earning a living, furnish excellent examples of the best that is being done in industrial education. The cities chosen for description are Gary, Chicago, and Cincinnati. This book is not concerned with schools or courses which are designed simply to give the pupils control of one specialized field of knowledge; that is, which train people for the processes of one particular industry or profession. It is true that most of the experiments in industrial education tried so far in this country have taken the material offered by the largest skilled industries of the neighborhood for their basis, and as a result have trained pupils for one or more definite trades. But wherever the experiment has been prompted by a sincere interest in education and in the welfare of the community this has not been the object of the work. The interest of the teachers is not centered on the welfare of any one industry, but on the welfare of the young people of the community. If the material prosperity of a community is due almost entirely to one or two industries, obviously the welfare of the individuals of the community is very closely connected with those industries. Then the educational purpose of training the children to the most intelligent use of their own capabilities and of their environment, is most easily served by using these industries as the material for the strictly utilitarian part of this training. The problem of general public-school education is not to train workers for a trade, but to make use of the whole environment of the child in order to supply motive and meaning to the work.

In Gary this has been done more completely than in any other single place. Superintendent Wirt believes firmly in the value of muscular and sense training for children; and instead of arranging artificial exercises for the purpose, he gives children the same sort of things to do that occupy their parents and call for muscular skill and fine coördination in the business of everyday life. Every child in Gary, boy and girl, has before his eyes in school finely equipped workshops, where he may, as soon as he is old

EDUCATION THROUGH INDUSTRY 253

enough, do his share of the actual work of running and keeping in order the school buildings. All of the schools except one small one where there are no high school pupils, have a lunch room where the girls learn to cook, and a sewing room where they learn to make their own clothes; a printing shop, and carpenter, electrical, machine, pattern, forging, and molding shops, where boys, and girls if they wish, can learn how most of the things that they see about them every day are made. There are painting departments, and a metal working room, and also bookkeeping and stenography classes. The science laboratories help give the child some understanding of the principles and processes at work in the world in which he lives.

The money and space required to equip and run these shops are saved from an ordinary sized school budget by the "two school system" that has been described above, and by the fact that all the expense usually charged by a school to repairs and paid out to contractors, is spent on these shops and for the salaries of the skilled workmen who teach in them. The buildings are kept in better repair than where all the work is done during the summer vacation, because as soon as anything needs to be fixed the pupils who are working in the shop that does that kind of work get at the repairs under the direction of the teacher. These shops can not be considered in any way an unnecessary luxury because they are used also by the high school pupils who are specializing for one kind of work and by the night and summer school for their vocational classes. The school management says in regard to the success of this plan, "When you have provided a plant where the children may live a complete life eight hours a day in work, study, and play, it is the simplest thing imaginable to permit the children in the workshops, under the direction and with the help of well-trained men and women, to assume the responsibility for the equipment and maintenance of the school plant. An industrial and commercial school for every child is thus provided without extra cost to the taxpayers."

The first three grades spend one hour a day in manual training and drawing, which take the form of simple hand-work and are not done in the shops, but in an especially equipped room with a trained teacher. The pupils draw, do painting and clay modeling, sewing and simple carpentry work. The five higher grades spend twice as much time on manual training and drawing. The little children go into the shops

Learning moulding, and manufacturing school equipment. (Gary, Ind.)

as helpers and watchers, much as they go into the science laboratories, and they pick up almost as much theory and understanding of processes as the older children possess. The art work and simpler forms of hand-work are kept up for the definite training in control and technique that comes from carrying through a problem independently. Because the small child's love of creating is very great, they continue until the pupils are old enough to choose what shop they will go into as apprentices to the teacher. Since sixth grade children are old enough and strong enough to begin doing the actual work of repairing and maintaining the building, in this grade they cease to be watchers and helpers and become real workers. Distributing school supplies, keeping the school records and taking care of the grounds are done by the pupils under the direction of the school office or the botanical laboratory, and constitute a course in shop-work just as much as does painting or repairing the electric lights. The school heat and power plant is also a laboratory for the pupils, in which they learn the principles of heating and lighting in a thoroughly practical way because they do much of the work connected with keeping the plant running.

The shop and science courses of the schools

last only a third of the year, and there is a shorter probation course of five weeks. The pupils choose with the advice of their teachers what shop course they will take; if at the end of five weeks they do not like it they may change. They must change twice during the year. In this way the work can not lose its educational character and become simply a method of making juvenile factory hands to do the school repairs. Taking three shop courses in one school year results in giving the pupil merely a superficial knowledge of the theory and processes of any one kind of work. But this is as it should be, for the pupils are not taking the courses to become carpenters, or electricians, or dressmakers, but to find out how the work of the world is done. Moving as they do from one thing to another they learn as much of the theory of the industry as children of their age can understand, while an all-around muscular and sense training is insured. To confine the growing child too long to the same kind of muscular activity is harmful both mentally and physically; to keep on growing he must have work which exercises his whole body, which presents new problems, keeps teaching him new things, and thus develops his powers of reasoning and judgment. Any manual labor ceases to be educative the moment it becomes thoroughly familiar and automatic.

In Gary, the child of the newly arrived immigrant from the agricultural districts of eastern Europe has as much chance to prepare for a vocation, that is really to learn his own capabilities for the environment in which he finds himself, as the child of the educated American. From the time he enters the public school system, whether day nursery, kindergarten, or first grade, he is among people who are interested in making him see things as they are, and in teaching him how to do things. In the nursery he has toys to play with which teach him to control his body; and he learns unconsciously, by being well taken care of, some of the principles of hygiene and right living. In the kindergarten the work to train his growing body to perform useful and accurate motions and coördination goes on. In the first three grades, emphasis is put on teaching him to read and write and obtain a good foundation for the theoretical knowledge which comes from books. His physical growth is taken care of on the playground, where he spends about two hours a day, doing things that develop his whole body in a natural way and playing games that give him opportunity to satisfy his desire to play. At the same time he is taking the first steps in a training which is more specifically vocational, in that it deals with the practical bread and butter side of life. He learns to handle the materials which lie at the foundations of civilization in much the same way that primitive people used them, because this way is suited to the degree of skill and understanding he has reached. On a little hand loom he weaves a piece of coarse cloth; with clay he makes dishes or other objects that are familiar to him; with reeds or raffia he makes baskets; and with pencil or paints he draws for the pleasure of making something beautiful; with needle and thread he makes himself a bag or apron. All these activities teach him the first steps in the manufacture of the things which are necessary to our life as we live it. The weaving and sewing show him how our clothing is made; the artistic turn that is given to all this work, through modeling and drawing, teach him that even the simplest things in life can be made beautiful, besides furnishing a necessary method of self-expression.

In the fourth grade the pupils stop the making of isolated things, the value of which lies entirely in the process of making, and where the thing's value lies solely in its interest to the child. They still have time, however, to train whatever artistic ability they may possess, and to develop through their music and art the esthetic side of their nature. But the rest of their hand-work takes a further vocational turn. The time for manual occupation is now all spent on intensive and useful work in some one kind of work or industry. These pupils are now less interested in games, so they spend less time playing and more time making things. The girl goes into the dressmaking department and learns to sew from the point of view of the worker who has to produce her own things. She is still too young to carry through a long, hard piece of work, so she goes for the first two years as a watcher and helper, listening to the lessons in theory that the seventh, eighth, or ninth grade pupils are taking, and helping them with their work. A girl may choose dressmaking for her first course, but at the end of three months she must change to some other department, perhaps helping cook the lunch for the school and learning about wholesome foods and food chemistry for the next three months. Or if she is fond of drawing, she may devote nearly all her time for shop work to developing her talent for that.

In the same way the boy chooses what shop he will go into for three months. In the carpenter shop he will be old enough really to make for himself some of the simpler things needed in the school building. If he choose the forging or casting shop he will have a chance to help at shoeing the horses for the use of the department of education, or to help an older boy make the mold for the iron stand to a school desk. In such ways he finds out something about the way iron is used for so many of our commonest things. In the fifth and sixth grades nearly all the boys try to get at least one course in store keeping. Here they go into the school storerooms with the janitor; and with the school lists at hand unpack and check up the material which comes in both from the workshops and from outside. Then as these things are needed through the building they take the requisitions from the office, distribute the material, and make the proper entries on the books. They are taught practical book-keeping and are responsible for the smooth running of the supply department while they are working there. As they learn the cost of all the material as well as the method of caring for it and distributing it, they get a good idea of the way a city spends its taxes and of the general business methods in use in stores. Both boys and girls may take a beginners' course in bookkeeping and office management. Here they go into what is called the school bank, and keep the records of the shop work of all the pupils in the school.

Before pupils can graduate from school they must have completed a certain number of hours of satisfactory work in the school shops. In order to fit the needs of every individual pupil, the amount of credit does not depend upon the mere attendance through a three months' course, but each pupil is given credit by the shop teacher for so many hours of work for the piece of work he has done. The rate of work is standardized, and thus a more equal training is insured for all, for the slow worker will get credit for only so much completed work regardless of the time it has taken him, and the fast worker will get credit for all he does even if he outstrips the average. A fixed number of "standard hours" of work entitle the pupil to "one credit," for which the pupil receives a credit certificate. When he has eight of these he has completed the work required by the vocational section of the Gary schools for graduation. All the work connected with keeping the records for these credit certificates is done by pupils under the direction of an advanced pupil.

From the seventh grade the pupils are the responsible workers in all the shops. A pupil who knows that he has to leave school when he has finished the eighth grade can now begin to specialize in the workrooms of some one department. If he wishes to become a printer he can work on the school presses for an entire year, or he can put in all his shop time in the bookkeeping department if he is attracted by office work. The girls begin to take charge of the lunch room, doing all the marketing and planning for the menus and keeping the books. Sewing work takes in more and more of the complications of the industry. The girls learn pattern drawing and designing, and may take a millinery course. The work for the students in office work is now extended to include stenography and typewriting and business methods. The art work also broadens to take in designing and hand metal work. There is no break between the work of the grades and the high school in the vocational department, except that as the pupil grows older he naturally tends to specialize toward what is to be his life work. The vocational department is on exactly the same level as the academic, and the school takes the wholesome attitude that the boy who intends to be a carpenter or painter needs to stay in school just as many years as the boy who is going to college. The result is the very high per cent. of pupils who go on to higher schools.

The ordinary view among children of laboring people in large cities is that only those who are going to be teachers need to continue at school after the age of fourteen; it does not make any difference that one is leaving to go into a factory or shop. But since the first day the Gary child began going to school he has seen boys and girls in their last year of high school still learning how to do the work that is being done where, perhaps, he expects ultimately to go to work. He knows that these pupils all have a tremendous advantage over him in the shop, that they will earn more, get a higher grade of work to do, and do it better. Through the theory lessons in the school shop he has a general idea of the scope and possibilities in his chosen trade, and what is more to the purpose, he knows how much more he has to learn about the work. He is familiar with the statistics of workers in that trade, knows the wages for the different degrees of skill and how far additional training can take a man. With all this information about, and outlook upon, his vocation it is not strange that so few, comparatively, of the pupils leave school, or that so many of those who have to leave come back for evening or Sunday classes.

The pupil who stays in a Gary school through

the four years of high school knows the purpose of the work he is doing, whether he is going to college or not. If he wants to go into office work, he shapes his course to that end, even before he gets his grammar grades diploma perhaps. But he is not taking any short cut to mere earning capacity in the first steps of office work. He is doing all the work necessary to give him the widest possible outlook. His studies include, of course, lessons in typewriting and stenography, bookkeeping and accounting, filing, etc.; but they include as well sufficient practice in English, grammar, and spelling so that he will be able to do his work well. They include work in history, geography and science, so that he will find his work interesting, and will have a background of general knowledge which will enrich his whole life. The student preparing for college does the work necessary for his entrance examinations, and a great deal of manual work besides, which most high school pupils are not supposed to have time for. It is just as valuable for the man who works with his brain to know how to do some of the things that the factory worker is doing, as it is for the latter to know how the patterns for the machine he is making were drawn, and the principles that govern the power supply in the factory. In

EDUCATION THROUGH INDUSTRY 265

Gary the work is vocational in all of these senses. Before the pupil leaves school he has an opportunity to learn the specific processes for any one of a larger number of professions. But from the first day he went to school he has been doing work that teaches the motives and principles of the uses to which the material world is put by his social environment, so that whatever work he goes into will really be a vocation, a calling in life, and not a mere routine engaged in only for the sake of pay.

The value of the pupils' training is greatly increased by the fact that all the work done is productive. All the shops are manufacturing plants for the Gary school; the business school finds a laboratory in the school office. In dressmaking or cooking the girls are making clothes which they need, or else cooking their own and other people's lunches. The science laboratories use the work of the shops for the illustration of their theories. The chemistry is the chemistry of food; botany and zoölogy include the care of the school grounds and animals. Drawing includes dress designing and house decoration, or pattern drawing for the hand metal shop. Arithmetic classes do the problems for their carpentry class, and English classes put emphasis on the things which the pupils say they need to know to work in the printing shop: usually paragraphing, spelling, and punctuation. The result of this coöperation is to make the book work better than if they put in all their time on books. The practical world is the real world to most people; but the world of ideas becomes intensely interesting when its connection with the world of action is clear. Because the work is real work constant opportunities are furnished to carry out the school policy of meeting the needs of the individual pupil. The classification according to fast, slow, and average workers, both in the vocational and academic departments, has already been described. It enables the pupil to do his work when he is ready for it, without being pushed ahead or held back by his fellow pupils; the slow worker may learn as much as the rapid worker, and the latter in turn does not develop shiftless habits because he has not enough to do. But if for any reason a pupil does not fit into any of the usual programs of classification, he is not forced to the conclusion that the school holds no place for him. The pupil who is physically unfit to sit at a desk and study goes to school, and spends all his time outdoors, with a teacher to help him get strong.

In the same way the two-school system enables the child who is weak in arithmetic to catch up without losing his standing in other subjects. He simply takes the arithmetic lessons with two grades. In the shops the poor pupil simply works longer on one thing, but as his progress is not bound up with that of the class it makes no difference. The pupil who thinks he hates school, or is too stupid to keep on going, is not dealt with by threats and punishments. His teachers take it for granted that there is something wrong with his program, and with his help fix it for him.

The child who hastens to leave school without any reason as soon as he may, is told that he may come back and spend all his time on the thing that he likes. This often results in winning back a pupil, for after he has worked for a few months in his favorite shop or the art room, he finds he needs more book knowledge to keep on there and so he asks to go back to his grade. The large number of foreign pupils is also more efficiently dealt with. The newcomer concentrates on English and reading and writing until he is able to go into the grade where his age would naturally place him, and the pupil who expects to go to school only a very short time before going to work can be put into the classes which will give him what he needs most, regardless of his age or grade. The work around the school buildings which can not be done by the pupils under the direction of the shop or department heads, is not done by outside hired help, but is given to some school pupil who is interested in that sort of work and is ready to leave school. This pupil holds the position for a few months only, until he has no more to learn from his work or gets a better position outside. These pupil assistants are paid slightly less than they could earn if they went into an office, but the plan often serves to keep a pupil under school influences and learning when he would otherwise have to leave school in order to earn money, perhaps just before he finishes his technical training.

Gary has fortunately been able to begin with such an all-around system of education, putting it into operation in all her schools in a nearly complete form, because the town was made, as it were, at a stroke and has grown rapidly from a waste stretch of sand dunes to a prosperous town. But many other cities are realizing more and more strongly the necessity of linking their curriculum more closely to the lives of their pupils, by furnishing the children with a general training and outlook on life which will fit them for their place in the world as adults.

Real work in a real shop begins in the fifth grade. (Gary, Ind.)

Recently the Chicago public schools have been introducing vocational work in some of the school buildings, while technical high schools give courses that are vocational, besides work in trade-training. Of course such elaborate equipment as that in Gary is impractical in a building where the shops are not used by the high school as well as the grades. Twenty or more of the regular school buildings in the city have been fitted up with carpenter shops and cooking and sewing rooms as well as laboratories for work in science. Each one of these schools has a garden where the pupils learn how to do practical city gardening. From one-fourth to even a half of the children's time is spent on manual training instead of one-eighth as in the other schools of the city, and in other respects the regular curriculum is being followed. The teachers in the schools who were there before the change of program feel convinced that the pupils not only get through with as much book work as they did when practically all their time was given to it, but that they actually do their work better because of the motive furnished by the hand work.

The courses given by the schools are not uniform, but most of the schools include courses in mechanical drawing, pattern making, metal work, woodwork, and printing for the boys, and for the girls, work in sewing, weaving, cooking, millinery, laundry, and general home-making. Both boys and girls have work in designing, pottery, bookbinding, and gardening. The program differs somewhat in different schools to meet the needs of the neighborhood or because of the resources of the building; but all the pupils of one school take the same work, so that when a pupil graduates from the eighth grade in one of these schools he has acquired a good beginner's knowledge of the principles and processes underlying two or three trades. This special work is supplemented by the regular work in music and art and this, with work in the elementary processes of sewing and weaving and pottery, constitutes the work for the younger grades. The object of this training is to enable the child to pick up the thread of life in his own community, by giving him an understanding of the elements of the occupations that supply man's daily needs; it is not to confine him to the industries of his neighborhood by teaching him some one skilled trade.

The laboratories for the study of the elements of science play a most important part in this work. In them the child learns to understand the foundations of modern industry, and so comes to his environment as a whole. Without this comprehensive vision no true vocational training can be successful, for it is only as he sees the place of different kinds of work and their relation to each other that the youth can truly choose what his own vocation is to be. Elementary courses in physics, chemistry, and botany are given pupils, and the bearing of the work on what they are doing in the shops is made clear. The botany is taught in connection with the gardening classes, chemistry for the girls is given in the form of the elements of food chemistry. One school gives a laboratory class in electricity, where the pupils make the industrial application of the laws they are studying, learning how to wire when they are learning about currents, and how to make a dynamo when they are working on magnets, etc. All the pupils take a course in the elements of science, so that they may get a true basis for their ideas about the way things work. There is no doubt that even in this rather tentative form the vocational schools have proved themselves a decided success, enabling pupils to do their book work better than before. Linking it with the things of everyday life gives it meaning and zest, and at the same time furnishes a mental and muscular control over the sort of thing they are going to need as adults while earning a living.

There are five technical high schools in Chicago, four for boys and one for girls. In all of these and in three other schools there are given what is known as "prevocational" courses. These are for pupils who have reached the legal age for leaving school, but who are so backward in their work that they ought not to be allowed to do so, while at the same time this backwardness makes them wish not to stay. These classes have proved again the great value of training for the practical things of everyday life to the city child. The boys and girls who are put into these classes are by no means deficient: they are simply children who for one reason or another have not been able to get along in the ordinary grade school as well as they ought; often the reason has been poor health, or because the child has had to move from one school to another, or simply because the usual curriculum made so little appeal that they were not able to hold themselves to the work. The prevocational classes include the sixth, seventh, and eighth grades, and give the greater part of the time to training the child through developing skill with his hands. Book work is not neglected, however, and the pupils are held up to the same standards that they would have to reach in an ordinary school, though they do not cover quite so much ground. The work can be made more varied than in the vocational grammar school because the equipment of the high school is available. Moreover, their ambition is so stimulated that very large numbers of them do additional work and transfer to the regular technical high school work, where in spite of their prior backwardness they do as well as the regular students. Ordinarily not a single one of them would ever have entered a high school.

The girls' technical high school does about what the vocational grammar schools are doing excepting that the work is more thorough, so that the graduate is more nearly prepared to take up work in some one industry. The cooking includes work in the school lunch room, and training in marketing, kitchen gardening and general housekeeping. The vocational classes proper take up large-quantity cooking, household administration, and restaurant management. In sewing the girls learn how to make their own clothes, but they learn as the work would have to be learned in a good dressmaking establishment; there is a course in machine operating for the girls who wish it. More advanced work teaches such principles of pattern making and designing as would be needed by a shop manager. But the most important difference is found in the emphasis that is put on the artistic side of women's traditional occupations. Drawing is taught while the girls are learning to design dresses, and color in the same way; how to make the home pleasing to the eye is made a vital problem in the housekeeping department, and the art department has decorated the model rooms. The pattern and coloring for any piece of work, whether it is a centerpiece to be embroidered, a dress, a piece of pottery, or weaving, has been carefully worked out in the art department by the worker herself before she begins upon it in the shop. The girls are not simply learning how to do the drudgery of housework more efficiently; they are learning how to lift it above drudgery by making it into a profession.

The vocational courses in the boys' technical high schools continue the pupils' study in the regular academic subjects, and give them work in excellently equipped shops. There is work in printing, carpentry, forging, metal work, mechanical drawing, and in the machine shop, well supplemented by the art department. The pupil does not specialize in one kind of work, but secures general training. The object of all the vocational courses in the grammar schools is to prepare the pupils for any branch of work that they may want to take up by giving them an outlook over all the branches of work carried on around them. The work is cultural in much the same way that it is cultural in Gary. The success of these courses in bringing boys back to school, in enabling others to catch up with their grade, and in keeping others in school, points strongly to the fact that for a great many pupils at least some work which will link their school course to the activities of everyday life is necessary.

The technical high schools give two-year courses for the pupils who can not afford to stay in school for four years. They are designed to give a boy training for a definite vocation, and are at the same time broad enough to count for the first two years of high school work if the boy should be able to go on later. At the Lane School two-year courses are given in patternmaking, machine shop work, carpentry, electricity, printing and mechanical drawing; all of these courses include work in English, shop arithmetic, drawing, and physiology. The four-year pupils take one of three courses, according to what they expect to do.

The technical course prepares students for college, the architectural course prepares for work in an architect's office, and the general trade course prepares for immediate entry into industry. During the first two years of work the student devotes his time to the study of general subjects, and during the last two the major part of his time is put in on work that leads directly to the vocation that he has chosen. The two-year course has not cut down the total attendance at the school by offering a short cut to pupils who would otherwise stay four years. On the contrary, it has drawn a different class of boys to school, those who had expected to go directly to work, but who were glad to make a sacrifice to stay on in school two years longer when an opportunity appeared to put those two years to definite account in training for the chosen occupation. All these technical high schools have shown conclusively that boys and girls like to go to school and like to learn, when they can see whither their lessons are leading. Giving the young work they want to do is a more effective method of keeping them in school than are truant officers or laws.

In the Lane School the work of the different departments is closely connected so that the pupils sees the relations of any one kind of work to everything he is doing. A problem being set to a group of students, such as the making of a gasoline engine or a vacuum cleaner, the different elements in its solution are worked out in the different classrooms. For the vacuum cleaner, for instance, the pupils must have reached a certain point in physics and electrical work before they are capable of trying to make the machine, since each pupil becomes in a sense the inventor, working out everything except the idea of the machine. When they are familiar with the principles which govern the cleaner they make rough sketches, which are discussed in the machine shop and altered until the sketch holds the promise of a practical result. In mechanical drawing, accurate drawings are made for the whole thing and for each part, from which patterns are made in the pattern shop. The pupils make their own molds and castings and when they have all the parts they construct the vacuum cleaner in the machine and electrical shops. The problem of the gasoline engine is worked out in a like way; and since all the work that is given the pupils has been chosen for its utility as well as its educational value, the pupil does everything connected with its production himself, from working out the theory in the laboratory or classroom to screwing the last bolt. The connection of theory and practice not only makes the former concrete and understandable, but it prevents the manual work from being routine and narrow. When a pupil has completed a problem of this sort he has increased knowledge and power. He has tested the facts he learned and knows what they stand for in terms of the use the world makes of them; and he has made a useful thing in a way which develops his own sense of independent intelligent power.

The attempts of the Cincinnati school board to give the school children of that city a better education, by giving them a better preparation for the future, have been made from a somewhat different point of view. Three-fourths of the school children of Cincinnati, as of so many other cities, leave school when they are fourteen years old; most of them do not go beyond the fifth grade. They do this because they feel they must go to work in order to give help at home. Of course a fifth-grade pupil of fourteen is fitted to do only the easiest and most mechanical work and so receives very low pay. Once at work in factory or shop on this routine kind of work, the chances for the worker to advance, or to become master of any trade, or branch of his trade, are slight. His schooling has given him only an elementary control of the three R's, and usually no knowledge of the theory or practice of the business he is engaged in. He soon finds himself in a position where he is not learning any more. It is only the very exceptional person who will go on educating himself and push ahead to a position of independence or responsibility under such conditions. The person who becomes economically swamped in the cheapest grades of work is not going to show much energy or intelligence in his life as citizen. The experiments of the Cincinnati schools in introducing manual and industrial training have been directed to remedying this evil by making the school work such that the pupil will desire to stay in school if this is in any way possible; and if it is not, by giving him opportunities to go on with his education while working.

The Ohio law requires children to stay in school until they are sixteen unless they must go to work, when they are given a certificate permitting them to work for the employer with whom they have found their first position. This permission must be renewed with each change of position. Consequently the pupil is kept in school until he has found work, and if for any reason he stops working, the school keeps in touch with him and can see that he goes back to school. The city also conducts continuation schools, where most of the pupils who leave between the ages of fourteen and sixteen have to return to school for a few hours a week, receiving theoretical instruction in the work they are doing. The cash girl has lessons in business English, arithmetic of the sort she has to use, and lessons in salesmanship, and receives a certain amount of general instruction about her special branch of trade. There are voluntary continuation classes for workers above sixteen years of age, by means of which any shop or store is able to use the facilities of the public schools to make their workers more efficient by giving them more knowledge of the theory of the trade.

These continuation classes are undoubtedly of the greatest value to the employee who can not go back to school, but they do not give him that grasp of present problems and conditions which would enable him intelligently to choose the work for which he is best suited. They improve him in a particular calling, but the calling may have been selected by accident. Their function is to make up to the child somewhat for what he has lost by having to become a wage earner so young. The coöperative plan which is being thoroughly tried out in Cincinnati is less of a makeshift and more of a distinct contribution to education, and has so far proved so successful as to be of great suggestive value. More than any other vocational plan it takes advantage of the educational value of the industries that are most important in the community. The factory shops of the city become the school shops for the pupils. Many of the big factories of the city have shown themselves willing to coöperate with the city for the first year of the experiment. This has proved so successful that many more factories are anxious to get their beginning workers in this way. In a sense it is a return to the old-fashioned apprenticeship method that prevailed when manufacturing was done by hand; for the pupils get their manual skill and the necessary practice in processes and shop conditions by working for wages in the city factories.

When the plan is further along the factories and stores will not be the only community institutions that will furnish laboratories for the school children of the city. The city college will begin its plan of having the domestic science pupils get their practice by working as nurses, cooks, housekeepers, or bookkeepers in the city hospital, and the engineering and architectural students will get theirs by working in the machine shops and draught-room of the city. As far as possible the departments of the city government will be used for the pupils' workshops; where they can not furnish opportunities for the kind of work the pupil needs, he will go into an office, store, or factory where conditions reach the standard set by the board of education. So far this plan has been tested only with the boys and girls who are taking the technical course in the city high schools. The pupils who have finished the first two years of work, which corresponds to the work of any good technical high school, begin working alternate weeks in shop and school. The pupil chooses a kind of work in which he wishes to specialize, and is then given a position in one of the factories or shops which are coöperating with the schools. He receives pay for his work as any beginner would, and does the regular work of the place, under the direction of, and responsible to, the shop superintendent. One week he works here under trade conditions, meeting the requirements of the place, the next week he returns to school, and his place in the factory is taken by another pupil who has chosen the same line of work. The week in school is devoted entirely to theoretical work. The pupil continues his work in English, history, mathematics, drawing, and science, and enriches his trade experience by a thorough study of the industry, all its processes and the science they involve, the use, history, and distribution of the goods, and the history of the industry. This alternation between factory and shop is kept up for the last two years of the course, and also during the pupil's college course, provided he goes on to a technical course in the city university.

From the standpoint of vocational guidance, this method has certain distinct advantages over having the pupil remain in the classroom until he goes into a shop permanently. His practical work in the factory is in the nature of an experiment. If his first choice proves a failure, the pupil does not get the moral setback that comes from a failure to the self-supporting person. The school takes the attitude that the pupil did not make the right choice; by coöperating with him, the effort is made to have his second factory experience correspond more nearly to his abilities and interest. A careful record of the pupil's work in the factory is kept as well as of his classroom work, and these two records are studied, not as separate items, but as interacting and inseparable. If his class work is good and his factory record poor, it is evident that he is in the wrong factory; and the nature of the class work will often give a hint of the sort of work to which the pupil ought to change. If all the work is mediocre, a change to another kind of practical work will often result in a marked improvement in the theoretical work if the change has been the right one. The pupil has an opportunity to test his own interests and abilities, to find if his judgment of them is correct; if it is not, he has a scientific basis on which to form a more correct judgment.

The work is not approached from the trade point of view; that is, the schools do not aim to turn out workers who have finished a two years' apprenticeship in a trade and are to that extent qualified as skilled workmen for that particular thing. The aim is to give the pupil some knowledge of the actual conditions in trade and industry so that he will have standards from which to make a final intelligent choice. The school work forms a necessary part of the training for this choice, for it is just as much a guide to the interests and bent of the boy as would be his success in any one shop. And it lifts his judgments from the plane of mere likes

Children are interested in the things they need to know about. (Gary, Ind.)

Making their own clothes in sewing class. (Gary, Ind.)

and dislikes to that of knowledge based on theory as well as practice. For the exceptional pupil who really knows what he wants, and is eager to go ahead with it, this plan offers distinct advantages. The boy's desire to get to work is satisfied by his weeks in the shop, and in his classroom he is learning enough of the larger aspects and possibilities of the trade to make him realize the value of additional theoretical training for the satisfaction of his own practical purposes.

As a result of the first year of working on this plan a large number of factories, at first indifferent to the plan, have asked to receive apprentices in this way, and a number of pupils have decided to go to college who, when they were spending all their time in school, had no such intention. The technical course for girls includes only those occupations that are traditionally supposed to belong to women because they are connected with home-making. They may continue for the four years working in school, which is made practical by having the pupils trim hats to wear, make their own clothes, do some commercial cooking, with the buying, selling, and bookkeeping connected with it; or they may specialize during the last two years as the boys do, by working alternate weeks in shop and school. So far girls have gone only into millinery or sewing establishments, where they work just as do the boys under actual trade conditions. The aim of the work for the girl, just as it is for the boy, is to help her find her life work, to fit herself for it mentally and morally, and to give her an intelligent attitude toward her profession and her community, using the shop experience not as an end in itself but a means to these larger ends.

CHAPTER XI

DEMOCRACY AND EDUCATION

THE schools that have been described were selected not because of any conviction that they represent all of the best work that is being done in this country, but simply because they illustrate the general trend of education at the present time, and because they seem fairly representative of different types of schools. Of necessity a great deal of material that would undoubtedly prove just as suggestive as what has been given, has been omitted. No attempt has been made to touch upon the important movement for the vitalization of rural education: a movement that is just as far reaching in its scope and wholesome in its aims as anything that is being done, since it purposes to overcome the disadvantages of isolation that have handicapped the country schoolteacher, and to make use of the natural environment of the child to give him a vocational education, in the same way that the city schools use their artificial environment. And except as their work illustrates a larger educational principle, very little attention has been given to the work of individual teachers or schools in their attempt to teach the conventional curriculum in the most efficient way. While devices and ingenious methods for getting results from pupils often seem most suggestive and even inspiring to the teacher, they do not fit into the plan of this book when they have to do simply with the better use of the usual material of the traditional education.

We have been concerned with the more fundamental changes in education, with the awakening of the schools to a realization of the fact that their work ought to prepare children for the life they are to lead in the world. The pupils who will pass this life in intellectual pursuits, and who get the necessary training for the practical side of their lives from their home environment, are such a small factor numerically that the schools are not acting wisely to shape all the work for them. The schools we have been discussing are all working away from a curriculum adapted to a small and specialized class towards one which shall be truly representive of the needs and conditions of a democratic society.

While these schools are all alike in that they reflect the new spirit in education, they differ greatly in the methods that have been developed to bring about the desired results; their surroundings and the class of pupils dealt with are varied enough to suggest the influence that local conditions must exercise over methods even when the aim is identical. To the educator for whom the problems of democracy are at all real, the vital necessity appears to be that of making the connection between the child and his environment as complete and intelligent as possible, both for the welfare of the child and for the sake of the community. The way this is to be accomplished will, of course, vary according to the conditions of the community and to a certain extent according to the temperament and beliefs of the educator. But great as the differences are between the different schools, between such a plan as that worked out by Mr. Meriam in Columbia, Missouri, and the curriculum of the Chicago public schools, an analysis of the ideas back of the apparent extreme divergence of views, reveals certain resemblances that seem more fundamental than the differences. The resemblances are more fundamental because they illustrate the direction that educational reform is taking, and because many of them are the direct result of the changes that modern science and psychology have brought about in our way of looking at the world.

Curiously enough most of these points of similarity are found in the views advocated by Rousseau, though it is only very recently that they have begun to enjoy anything more than a theoretical respect. The first point of similarity is the importance that is accorded to the physical welfare of the pupils. The necessity of insuring the health of all young people as the foundation on which to build other qualities and abilities, and the hopelessness of trying to build where the body is weak, ill-nourished, or uncontrolled, is now so well recognized that it has become a commonplace and needs only a passing mention here. Health is as important from the social point of view as from the individual, so that attention to it is doubly necessary to a successful community.

While all schools realize the importance of healthy pupils, the possibilities of using the activities of the child that are employed in giving him a strong healthy body, for general educational purposes, are not so well understood. As yet it is the pioneer in education who realizes the extent to which young children learn through the use of their bodies, and the impossibility of insuring general intelligence through a system which does not use the body to teach the mind and the mind to teach the body. This is simply a restatement of Rousseau's proposition that the education of the young child rests largely on whether he is allowed to "develop naturally" or not. It has already been pointed out to what an extent Mrs. Johnson depends on the physical growth of her pupils as a tool for developing their intellectual ability, as well as the important part that muscular skill plays in the educational system of Madame Montessori. This seems not only reasonable but necessary when we think of the mere amount of movement, handling, and feeling of things that a baby must indulge in to understand the most familiar objects in its environment, and remember that the child and the adult learn with the same mental machinery as the very small child. There is no difference in the way the organism works after it is able to talk and walk; the difference lies in the greater complexity of activities which is made possible by the preliminary exercises. Modern psychology has pointed out the fact that the native instincts of a human being are his tools for learning. Instincts all express themselves through the body; therefore education which stifles bodily activities, stifles instincts, and so prevents the natural method of learning. To the extent of making an educational application of this fact, all the schools described are using the physical activities of their pupils, and so the means of their physical development, as instruments for training powers of judgment and right thinking. That is to say the pupils are learning by doing. Aside from the psychological reasons for teaching by this method, it is the logical consequence of a realization of the importance of the physical welfare of the child, and necessarily brings changes in the material of the schoolroom.

What are the pupils to do in order to learn? Mere activity, if not directed toward some end, may result in developing muscular strength, but it can have very little effect on the mental development of the pupils. These schools have all answered the question in the same general way, though the definite problems on which they work differ. The children must have activities which have some educative content, that is, which reproduce the conditions of real life. This is true whether they are studying about things that happened hundreds of years ago or whether they are doing problems in arithmetic or learning to plane a board. The historical facts which are presented must be true, and whether the pupils are writing a play based on them or are building a viking boat, the details of the work as well as the main idea must conform to the known facts. When a pupil learns by doing he is reliving both mentally and physically some experience which has proved important to the human race; he goes through the same mental processes as those who originally did these things. Because he has done them he knows the value of the result, that is, the fact. A statement, even of facts, does not reveal the value of the fact, or the sense of its truth—of the fact that it is a fact. Where children are fed only on book knowledge, one "fact" is as good as another; they have no standards of judgment or belief. Take the child studying weights and measures; he reads in his text-book that eight quarts make a peck, but when he does examples he is apt, as every schoolteacher knows, to substitute four for eight. Evidently the statement as he read it in the book did not stand for anything that goes on outside the book, so it is a matter of accident what figure lodges in his brain, or whether any does. But the grocer's boy who has measured out pecks with a quart measure *knows*. He has made pecks; he would laugh at anybody who suggested that four quarts made a peck. What is the difference in these two cases? The schoolboy has a result without the activity of which it is the result. To the grocer's boy the statement has value and truth, for it is the obvious result of an experience—it is a *fact*.

Thus we see that it is a mistake to suppose that practical activities have only or even mainly a utilitarian value in the schoolroom. They are necessary if the pupil is to understand the facts which the teacher wishes him to learn; if his knowledge is to be real, not verbal; if his education is to furnish standards of judgment and comparison. With the adult it is undoubtedly true that most of the activities of practical life have become simply means of satisfying more or less imperative wants. He has performed them so often that their meaning as types of human knowledge has disappeared. But with the school child this is not true. Take a child in the school kitchen; he is not merely preparing that day's midday meal because he must eat; he is learning a multitude of new things. In following the directions of the *recipe* he is learning accuracy, and the success or failure of the dish serves as an excellent measure of the pupil's success. In measuring quantities he is learning arithmetic and tables of measures; in mixing materials, he is finding out how substances act when they are manipulated; in baking or boiling he is discovering some of the elementary facts of physics and chemistry. Repetition of these acts by adults, after the muscular and intellectual mastery of the adjustments they call for has been established, gives the casual thinker the impression that pupils also are doing no more than wasting their time on insignificant things. The grocer's boy knows what a peck is because he has used it to measure things with, but since his stock of knowledge is not increased as he goes on measuring out peck after peck, the point is soon reached where intellectual discovery ends and mere performance of a task takes its place. This is the point where the school can see that the pupil's intellectual growth continues; while the activity of the mere worker who is doing the thing for its immediate practical use becomes mechanical. The school says the pupil has had enough of this particular experience; he knows how to do this thing when he needs to and he has understood the principles or facts which it illustrates; it is time he moved on to other experiences which will teach him other values and facts. When the pupil has learned how to follow a recipe, how to handle foodstuffs and use the stove he does not go on repeating the same elementary steps; he begins to extend his work to take in the larger aspects of cooking. The educative value of the cooking lessons continues because he is now studying questions of food values, menus, the cost of food, and the chemistry of food stuffs, and cooking. The kitchen becomes a laboratory for the study of a fundamental factor in human life.

The moral advantages of an active form of education reënforce its intellectual benefits. We have seen how this method of teaching necessitates greater freedom for the pupil, and that this freedom is a positive factor in the intellectual and moral development of the pupils. In the same way the substitution of practical activities for the usual isolated text-book study achieves positive moral results which are marked to any teacher who has used both methods. Where the accumulation of facts presented in books is the standard, memory must be relied upon as the principal tool for acquiring knowledge. The pupil must be stimulated to remember facts; it makes comparatively little difference whether he has to remember them in the exact words of the book, or in his own words, for in either case the problem is to see that he does store up information. The inevitable re-

Training the hand, eye, and brain by doing useful work. (Gary, Ind.)

sult is that the child is rewarded when his memory is successful, and punished by failure and low marks when it is not successful. The emphasis shifts from the importance of the work that is done to the pupil's degree of external success in doing it. Since no one's performance is perfect, the failures become the obvious and emphasized thing. The pupil has to fight constantly against the discouragement of never reaching the standard he is told he is expected to reach. His mistakes are constantly corrected and pointed out. Such successes as he achieves are not especially inspiring because he does no more than reproduce the lesson as it already exists in the book. The virtues that the good scholar will cultivate are the colorless, negative virtues of obedience, docility, and submission. By putting himself in an attitude of complete passivity he is more nearly able to give back just what he heard from the teacher or read in the book.

Rewards and high marks are at best artificial aims to strive for; they accustom children to expect to get something besides the value of the product for work they do. The extent to which schools are compelled to rely upon these motives shows how dependent they are upon motives which are foreign to truly moral activity. But in the schools where the children are getting their knowledge by doing things, it is presented to them through all their senses and carried over into acts; it needs no feat of memory to retain what they find out; the muscles, sight, hearing, touch, and their own reasoning processes all combine to make the result part of the working equipment of the child. Success gives a glow of positive achievement; artificial inducements to work are no longer necessary, and the child learns to work from love of the work itself, not for a reward or because he is afraid of a punishment. Activity calls for the positive virtues—energy, initiative, and originality—qualities that are worth more to the world than even the most perfect faithfulness in carrying out orders. The pupil sees the value of his work and so sees his own progress, which spurs him on to further results. In consequence his mistakes do not assume undue importance or discourage him. He can actively use them as helps in doing better next time. Since the children are no longer working for rewards, the temptation to cheat is reduced to the minimum. There is no motive for doing dishonest acts, since the result shows whether the child has done the work, the only end recognized. The moral value of working for the sake of what is being done is certainly higher than that of working for rewards; and while it is possible that a really bad character will not be reformed by being placed in a situation where there is nothing to be gained excepting through an independent and energetic habit of work, the weak character will be strengthened and the strong one will not form any of those small bad habits that seem so unimportant at first and that are so serious in their cumulative effect.

Another point that most of the present day reformers have in common, in distinction from the traditional way of looking at school work, is the attempt to find work of interest to the pupils. This used to be looked at as a matter of very little importance; in fact a certain amount of work that did not interest was supposed to be a very good thing for the moral character of the pupil. This work was supposed to have even greater disciplinary qualities than the rest of the work. Forcing the child to carry through a task which did not appeal to him was supposed to develop perseverance and strength of character. There is no doubt that the ability to perform an irksome duty is a very useful accomplishment, but the usefulness does not lie in the irksomeness of the task. Things are not useful or necessary because they are unpleasant or tiresome, but in spite of these characteristics. The habit of giving work to pupils solely for the sake of its "disciplinary" value would seem to indicate a blindness to moral values rather than an excess of moral zeal, for after all the habit is little more than holding up a thing's defects as its virtues.

But if lack of interest is not to be admitted as a motive in selection of class work, it is fair enough to object that interest can not serve as a criterion, either. If we take interest in its narrowest sense, as meaning something which amuses and appeals to the child because of its power of entertainment, the objection has truth. The critic of the new spirit in education is apt to assume that this narrow sense is what is meant when he hears that the pupils ought to be interested in what they are doing. Then logically enough he goes on to point out that such a system lacks moral fiber, that it caters to the whims of children, and is in reality an example of the general softening of the social fiber, of every one's desire for the easy way. But the work is not made easy for the pupils; nor yet is there any attempt to give the traditional curriculum a sugar coating. The change is of a more fundamental character and is based on sound psychological theory. The work given to the children has changed; the attempt is not to make all the child's tasks interesting to him, but to select work on the basis of the natural appeal it makes to the child. Interest ought to be the basis for selection because children are interested in the things they need to learn.

Every one is familiar with the way a baby will spend a long time making over and over again the same motions or feeling of some object, and of the intense interest children two and three years old take in building a tower of blocks, or filling a pail with sand. They do it not once but scores of times, and always with the same deep absorption, for it is real work to them. Their growing, unformed muscles have not yet learned to act automatically; every motion that is aimed at something must be repeated under the conscious direction of the child's mind until he can make it without being aware of effort towards an adjustment. Since the little child must adjust the things about him, his interests and his needs are identical; if they were not he could not live. As a child grows older his control over his immediate needs so rapidly becomes automatic, that we are apt to forget that he still learns as the baby does. The necessary thing is still, as it will be all his life, the power of adjustment. Good adjustment means a successful human being, so that instinctively we are more interested in learning these adjustments than in anything else. Now the child is interested in adjusting himself through physical activity to the things he comes up against, because he must master his physical environment to live. The things that are of interest to him are the things that he needs to work on. It is then the part of wisdom in selecting the work for any group of children, to take it from that group of things in the child's environment which is arousing their curiosity and interest at that time. Obviously as the child grows older and his control of his body and physical environment increases he will reach out to the more complicated and theoretical aspects of the life he sees about him.

But in just this same way the work in the classroom reaches out to include facts and events which do not belong in any obvious way to the child's immediate environment. Thus the range of the material is not in any way limited by making interest a standard for selection. Work that appeals to pupils as worth while, that holds out the promise of resulting in something to their own interests, involves just as much persistence and concentration as the work which is given by the sternest advocate of disciplinary drill. The latter requires the pupil to strive for ends which he can not see, so that he has to be kept at the task by means of offering artificial ends, marks, and promotions, and by isolating him in an atmosphere where his mind and senses are not being constantly besieged by the call of life which appeals so strongly to him. But the pupil presented with a problem, the solution of which will give him an immediate sense of accomplishment and satisfied curiosity, will bend all his powers to the work; the end itself will furnish the stimulus necessary to carry him through the drudgery.

The conventional type of education which trains children to docility and obedience, to the careful performance of imposed tasks because they are imposed, regardless of where they lead, is suited to an autocratic society. These are the traits needed in a state where there is one head to plan and care for the lives and institutions of the people. But in a democracy they interfere with the successful conduct of society and government. Our famous, brief definition of a democracy, as "government of the people, for the people and by the people," gives perhaps the best clew to what is involved in a democratic society. Responsibility for the conduct of society and government rests on every member of society. Therefore, every one must receive a training that will enable him to meet this responsibility, giving him just ideas of the condition and needs of the people collectively, and developing those qualities which will insure his doing a fair share of the work of government. If we train our children to take orders, to do things simply because they are told to, and fail to give them confidence to act and think for themselves, we are putting an almost insurmountable obstacle in the way of overcoming the present defects of our system and of establishing the truth of democratic ideals. Our State is founded on freedom, but when we train the State of to-morrow, we allow it just as little freedom as possible. Children in school must be allowed freedom so that they will know what its use means when they become the controlling body, and they must be allowed to develop active qualities of initiative, independence, and resourcefulness, before the abuses and failures of democracy will disappear.

The spread of the realization of this connection between democracy and education is perhaps the most interesting and significant phase of present educational tendencies. It accounts for the growing interest in popular education, and constitutes a strong reënforcement to the arguments of science and psychology for the changes which have been outlined. There is no doubt that the text-book method of education is well suited to that small group of children who by environment are placed above the necessity of engaging in practical life and who are at the same time interested in abstract ideas. But even for this type of person the system leaves great gaps in his grasp of knowledge; it gives no place to the part that action plays in the development of intelligence, and it trains along the lines of the natural inclinations of the student and does not develop the practical qualities which are usually weak in the abstract person. For the great majority whose interests are not abstract, and who have to pass their lives in some practical occupation, usually in actually working with their hands, a method of education is necessary which bridges the gap between the purely intellectual and theoretical sides of life and their own occupations. With the spread of the ideas of democracy, and the accompanying awakening to social problems, people are beginning to realize that every one, regardless of the class to which he happens to belong, has a right to demand an education which shall meet his own needs, and that for its own sake the State must supply this demand.

Until recently school education has met the needs of only one class of people, those who are interested in knowledge for its own sake, teachers, scholars, and research workers. The idea that training is necessary for the man who works with his hands is still so new that the schools are only just beginning to admit that control of the material things of life is knowledge at all. Until very recently schools have neglected the class of people who are numerically the largest and upon whom the whole world depends for its supply of necessities. One reason for this is the fact that democracy is a comparatively new thing in itself; and until its advent, the right of the majority, the very people who work with their hands, to supply any of their larger spiritual needs was never admitted. Their function, almost their reason for existence, was to take care of the material wants of the ruling classes.

Two great changes have occurred in the last century and a half which have altered men's habits of living and of thinking. We have just seen how one of these, the growth of democratic ideals, demands a change in education. The other, the change that has come about through scientific discoveries, must also be reflected in the classroom. To piece together all one's historical information into a rough picture of society before the discovery of the steam engine and of electricity, will hardly serve to delineate sufficiently the changes in the very fundamentals of society that these and similar discoveries have brought about. The one possibly most significant from the point of view of education is the incredible increase in the number of facts that must be part of the mental furniture of any one who meets even the ordinary situations of life successfully. They are so many that any attempt to teach them all from text-books in school hours would be simply ridiculous. But the schools instead of facing this frankly and then changing their curriculum so that they could teach pupils how to learn from the world itself, have gone on bravely teaching as many facts as possible. The changes made have been in the way of inventing schemes that would increase the consumption of facts. But the change that is demanded by science is a more radical one; and as far as it has been worked out at present it follows the general lines that have been suggested in this book. This includes, as the curricula of these different schools have shown, not alone teaching of the scientific laws that have brought about the changes in society since their discovery, but the substitution of real work which itself teaches the facts of life for the study and memorization of facts after they have been classified in books.

If schools are to recognize the needs of all classes of pupils, and give pupils a training that will insure their becoming successful and valuable citizens, they must give work that will not only make the pupils strong physically and morally and give them the right attitude towards the state and their neighbors, but that will as well give them enough control over their material environment to enable them to be economically independent. Preparation for the professions has always been taken care of; it is, as we have seen, the future of the worker in industry which has been neglected. The complications of modern industry due to scientific discoveries make it necessary for the worker who aspires to real success to have a good foundation of general education on which to build his technical skill, and the complications of human nature make it equally necessary that the beginner shall find his way into work that is suited to his tastes and abilities. A discussion of general educational principles is concerned only with industrial or vocational education which supplies these two needs. The questions of specific trade and professional training fall wholly outside the scope of this book. However, certain facts connected with the movement to push industrial training in its narrower sense have a direct bearing on the larger question. For there is great danger just at present that, as the work spreads, the really educative type of work that is being done in Gary and Chicago may be overlooked in favor of trade training.

The attention of influential citizens is more easily focused on the need of skilled workers than on that of a general educational readjustment. The former is brought home to them by their own experience, perhaps by their self-interest. They are readily impressed with the extent to which Germany has made technical trade training a national asset in pushing the commercial rivalries of that empire. Nothing seems so direct and practical as to establish a system of continuation schools to improve workers between the ages of fourteen and eighteen who have left school at the earliest age, and to set up separate schools which shall prepare directly for various lines of shop work, leaving the existing schools practically unchanged to prepare pupils for higher schools and for the walks of life where there is less manual work.

Continuation schools are valuable and important, but only as palliatives and makeshifts; they deal with conditions which ought not to exist. Children should not leave school at fourteen, but should stay in school until they are sixteen or eighteen, and be helped to an intelligent use of their energies and to the proper choice of work. It is a commonplace among teachers and workers who come in contact with any number of pupils who leave school at fourteen to go to work, that the reason is not so much financial pressure as it is lack of conviction that school is doing them any good. Of course there are cases where the child enjoys school but is forced to leave at the first opportunity in order to earn money. But even in these rare instances it would usually be wiser to continue the family arrangements that were in vogue up to the child's fourteenth birthday, even if they include charity. The wages of the child of fourteen and fifteen are so low that they make a material difference only to the family who is already living on an inadequate scale.

The hopelessness of the situation is increased by the fact that these children increase their earning capacity much more slowly and reach as their maximum a much lower level than the child who is kept in school, so that in the long run the loss both to the child and his family more than offsets the precarious temporary gain. But the commonest reason advanced by pupils for leaving school is that they did not like it, and were anxious to get some real work to do. Not that they were prepared to go to work, or had finished any course of training, but simply that school seemed so futile and satisfied so few of their interests that they seized the first opportunity to make a change to something that seemed more real, something where there was a visible result.

What is needed then is a reorganization of the ordinary school work to meet the needs of this class of pupils, so that they will wish to stay in school for the value of what they are learning. The present system is bungling and short-sighted; continuation schools patch up some of its defects; they do not overcome them, nor do they enable the pupils to achieve a belated intellectual growth, where the maladjustment of the elementary school has served to check it. The ideal is not to use the schools as tools of existing industrial systems, but to use industry for the reorganization of the schools.

There is danger that the concentrated interests of business men and their influential activity in public matters will segregate training for industry to the damage of both democracy and education. Educators must insist upon the primacy of educational values, not in their own behalf, but because these represent the more fundamental interests of society, especially of a society organized on a democratic basis. The place of industry in education is not to hurry the preparation of the individual pupil for his individual trade. It should be used (as in the Gary, Indianapolis, and other schools) to give practical value to the theoretical knowledge that every pupil should have, and to give him an understanding of the conditions and institutions of his environment. When this is done the pupil will have the necessary knowledge and intelligence to make the right choice of work and to direct his own efforts towards getting the necessary technical skill. His choice will not be limited by the fact that he already knows how to do one thing and only one; it will be dictated only by his own ability and natural aptitude.

The trade and continuation schools take their pupils before they are old enough or have knowledge enough of their own power to be able to make a wise choice, and then they drill them in one narrow groove, both in their theoretical work and in their manual skill, so that the pupil finds himself marked for one occupation only. If it proves not to be the right one for him it is still the only one he is trained for. Such a system does not give an opportunity for the best development of the individual's abilities, and it tends to keep people fixed in classes.

The very industries that seem to benefit most by receiving skilled workers for the first steps of the trade will lose by it in the more difficult processes, for the workers will not have the background of general knowledge and wider experience that the graduate of a technical high school or vocational school should have acquired. But the introduction of the material of occupations into the schools for the sake of the control of the environment brought by their use will do much to give us the proportion of independent, intelligent citizens that are needed in a democracy.

It is fatal for a democracy to permit the formation of fixed classes. Differences of wealth, the existence of large masses of unskilled laborers, contempt for work with the hands, inability to secure the training which enables one to forge ahead in life, all operate to produce classes, and to widen the gulf between them. Statesmen and legislation can do something to combat these evil forces. Wise philanthropy can do something. But the only fundamental agency for good is the public school system. Every American is proud of what has been accomplished in the past in fostering among very diverse elements of population a spirit of unity and of brotherhood so that the sense of common interests and aims has prevailed over the strong forces working to divide our people into classes. The increasing complexity of our life, with the great accumulation of wealth at one social extreme and the condition of almost dire necessity at the other makes the task of democracy constantly more difficult. The days are rapidly passing when the simple provision of a system in which all individuals mingle is enough to meet the need. The subject-matter and the methods of teaching must be positively and aggressively adapted to the end.

There must not be one system for the children of parents who have more leisure and another for the children of those who are wage-earners. The physical separation forced by such a scheme, while unfavorable to the development of a proper mutual sympathy, is the least of its evils. Worse is the fact that the over bookish education for some and the over "practical'' education for others brings about a division of mental and moral habits, ideals and outlook.

The academic education turns out future citizens with no sympathy for work done with the hands, and with absolutely no training for understanding the most serious of present day social and political difficulties. The trade training will turn future workers who may have greater immediate skill than they would have had without their training, but who have no enlargement of mind, no insight into the scientific and social significance of the work they do, no education which assists them in finding their way on or in making their own adjustments. A division of the public school system into one part which pursues traditional methods, with incidental improvements, and another which deals with those who are to go into manual labor means a plan of social predestination totally foreign to the spirit of a democracy.

The democracy which proclaims equality of opportunity as its ideal requires an education in which learning and social application, ideas and practice, work and recognition of the meaning of what is done, are united from the beginning and for all. Schools such as we have discussed in this book—and they are rapidly coming into being in large numbers all over the country—are showing how the ideal of equal opportunity for all is to be transmuted into reality.

NORTHERN ILLINOIS UNIVERSITY
3 1211 00660012 2